INTIMATE JUSTICE

INTIMATE JUSTICE

The Black Female Body and the Body Politic

Shatema Threadcraft

OXFORD
UNIVERSITY PRESS

OXFORD
UNIVERSITY PRESS

Oxford University Press is a department of the University of Oxford. It furthers the University's objective of excellence in research, scholarship, and education by publishing worldwide. Oxford is a registered trade mark of Oxford University Press in the UK and certain other countries.

Published in the United States of America by Oxford University Press
198 Madison Avenue, New York, NY 10016, United States of America.

Library of Congress Cataloging-in-Publication Data
Names: Threadcraft, Shatema, author.
Title: Intimate justice : the black female body and the body politic /
Shatema Threadcraft.
Description: New York, NY : Oxford University Press, [2016] |
Includes bibliographical references and index.
Identifiers: LCCN 2016006849 (print) | LCCN 2016014054 (ebook) |
ISBN 9780190251635 (hardcover) | ISBN 9780190251659 (Updf)
Subjects: LCSH: African American women—Social conditions. |
African American women—Violence against. | Sex crimes—United States. |
Feminism—United States. | Equality—United States. |
United States—Race relations.
Classification: LCC E185.86 .T448 2016 (print) | LCC E185.86 (ebook) |
DDC 305.48/896073—dc23
LC record available at http://lccn.loc.gov/2016006849

CONTENTS

PREFACE

Elaine Riddick stood before the governor's task force in 2011 and asked what the assembled committee thought her life was worth. The question of what her reproductive life was worth, however, had actually been answered on March 5, 1968—it was worthless. That day, the day a fourteen-year-old Riddick delivered her son Tony, a physician carried out the North Carolina Eugenics Board's (NCEB's) order that she be sterilized.

Riddick's pregnancy was the result of rape; she had actually been kidnapped and raped. She grew up in an area of North Carolina nicknamed "Little Korea," so nicknamed, legend has it, because conditions there—the violence and poverty—mimicked conditions in a war-torn developing nation. Days before the surgery welfare officials informed Riddick's grandmother that she must "consent" to the procedure or the family would no longer receive state assistance. What a choice.

Years later, when Riddick learned of what had happened—after her failure to conceive ended a marriage, after severe depression and "hibernation" in the face of her friends' pregnancies—her sister suggested that she do something about it. Riddick contacted the Women's Rights Project of the American Civil Liberties Union

(ACLU). The organization was searching for plaintiffs in a class-action suit against the NCEB. Research revealed that the board had ordered the "operation for sterilization and asexualization" 7,600 times in its fifty-five-year run.

The North Carolina General Assembly created the NCEB in 1933, charging the board with reviewing the sterilization of "feebleminded" and epileptic patients. In the 1930s, an era in which there were few population-related fears regarding blacks, only 23 percent of those sterilized were black; by the 1950s, however, due to white anxieties regarding supporting blacks on welfare, welfare department heads increasingly saw sterilization as an option for reducing welfare expenditures.[1] Between 1964 and 1966 there was a dramatic shift in the racial makeup of those the board targeted, as the percentage of blacks sterilized rose to 64 in this period. By the end of its run the board's orders for sterilization evinced profound racial bias, as 68 percent of its victims were black women.

Riddick went on to join the ACLU's class action and in 1974 the Women's Rights Project filed suit against the board in federal court. Ten years later, after forty-five minutes of deliberation, a jury decided that Riddick had not been "unlawfully deprived of her right to bear children."

But she has never given up.

In June 2011, forty-three years after that fateful day, she stood before the governor's task force and demanded justice. But what, in this instance, does justice require?

Riddick's recent testimony helps to illustrate the fact that the project of intimate racial justice—the project of providing blacks their due in the sphere of intimate relations—is incomplete; she and others demanded justice in our time. And though Riddick and her fellow NCEB victims were offered small sums by way of restitution, her story also highlights the apparent inadequacy of redistributive redress alone for what she suffered. Riddick herself makes this clear. Of the $50,000 compensation the Governor's Eugenics Compensation Taskforce offered her so many years later, she says, "Is that what they think my life is worth? How much are the kids I never had worth? $50,000 is not enough to bury my pain."[2]

The NCEB has been widely discredited, as have eugenic steriliza-tions full stop. Does this mean that women like Riddick will no longer be deprived of their right to bear and rear children? Again, Riddick herself would say no.

Riddick is now an advocate for black women's reproductive rights as well as for greater security provision for black women and girls. She serves as the executive director of the Rebecca Project for Justice, she is an expert on Depo-Provera, and she continues to fight against what she sees as new iterations of what she experienced.[3] For example, she served as the victims' coordinator in a Depo-Provera class-action lawsuit. Her organization, the Rebecca Project, holds that the distribution of Depo-Provera is an issue of racial justice, as the drug is profoundly unevenly distributed across the global North/ South divide. United Nations data indicates, for example, that it is rarely used by white and affluent women in America and Europe.

And what of the violent and impoverished conditions that facili-tated the thirteen-year-old Riddick's initial kidnapping and sexual assault? The condition in which she found herself—an institutional spatial context that denied adequate security provision to blacks—was no product of mere drift.

Riddick is tackling this issue as well. Beyond her contraception and population-control related work, she is working to transform the broader conditions that facilitated her sexual assault. She is build-ing the Elaine Riddick Sister Sanctuary for at-risk girls in Georgia—girls who are potential victims of sex trafficking or who are pregnant without a place to call home. Riddick is working to intervene in what President Obama recently called the "sexual-assault-to-prison pipe-line" that many young black women in the United States are funneled through.[4]

Sadly, for many black women and girls the conditions in which a young Riddick found herself remain and have, in many instances, only been made worse by the rise of the so-called "carceral state."

For example, in *Arrested Justice: Violence and America's Prison Nation*, Beth Richie documents several black women's experience of physical and sexual violence—from intimate partners, community members, and the police—in what she calls America's "prison nation." Richie tells the story of Ms. B, a fifty-year-old mother living in a Chicago public housing project slated for demolition in a "transitioning neighborhood." Years earlier she had been active in groups that organized to resist the demolition of public housing, the Chicago Housing Authority's "Plan for Transformation" in the late 1990s and early 2000s, but was not an active member at the time of the following assault:

> On the evening of the first attack, the five undercover officers, three with guns drawn, accosted Ms. B outside of her building and demanded that she give them her apartment keys. The officers then forced Ms. B into the one working elevator and, when the door opened on her floor, pushed her inside the apartment. They then proceeded to ransack her home, throwing her belongings around and breaking precious objects (like a picture of a brown-skinned Jesus) while they cursed and threatened her, referring to her in sexually and racially demeaning terms like "nigger-cunt-bitch." Three of the officers broke down the door to her 19-year-old son's bedroom and ordered him and a visiting friend to lie face down on the floor while they handcuffed them. Three officers took turns punching and kicking them for more than 30 minutes before taking them forcibly out of the apartment. In response to Ms. B's pleas for mercy for the young men, the two police officers who remained in the apartment led her to the bathroom, ordered her to remove all of her clothing, to lie down on the floor, to spread her legs, and to effectively do an internal cavity search on herself while they stood over her and watched. . . . By the time the police officers left the ransacked apartment, Ms. B was physically battered, naked, emotionally traumatized, and terrified about where and how her son and his

friend were.... That occurred on April 13, 2003. Over the next three months, this same group of rogue police officers (all white, all men, and all young) assaulted Ms. B six times. The brutality included physical beatings, sexual harassment and stalking, destruction of her personal property, and threats to members of her family who were particularly vulnerable because they were on parole or probation (and subsequently at risk of re-arrest at the whim of the police).[5]

Ms. B had been gang-raped twice before this incident and Richie says it was easy for her to draw the parallels between these experiences and her assaults by police officers.

Riddick works to ensure that black women and girls do not face what she faced, but the job is not hers alone. Richie writes that gender-based violence prevention activists and black community organizations have long failed women like Ms. B, but the job is not theirs alone.

Intimate Justice considers the ways in which the black female body—bodies like Riddick's—as well as the capacities of the black body most closely associated with femininity and the material labors that typically fall to women have been constrained and diminished within the American body politic. It also examines the ways in which the black female body, in particular, has been subject to disproportionate violence under conditions of racial inequality. It examines the above in an effort to put forward a theory of corrective racial justice that adequately accounts for black women's experiences of racial domination at key points in American history and responds to black women's pressing contemporary justice concerns—I distinguish this most pointedly from the exploitation of and violence wrought against the black body most closely associated with the control and use of the black male body under racial domination—in order to outline what we all owe to Riddick and the women she would aid and protect, what we owe to Ms. B and women like her. In an effort to accomplish the above the book brings together the insights of black feminist thinkers and feminist political theorists, both the latter's revisions of key concepts in political theory as well as their critiques of the deficiencies of mainstream modern thinkers' conceptions of the modern body politic—to consider the place—past, present, and future—of the black female body in the body politic.

INTIMATE JUSTICE

[1]

INTRODUCTION

Black Female Body Politics

Historically, black women have identified work in the context of family as humanizing labor, work that affirms their identity as women, as human beings showing love and care, the very gesture of humanity white supremacist ideology claimed black people were incapable of expressing.

—bell hooks, Feminist Theory from Margin to Center[1]

Some problems we share as women and some we do not. You fear your children will grow up to join the patriarchy and testify against you; we fear our children will be dragged from a car and shot down in the street and you will turn your backs upon the reasons they are dying.

—Audre Lorde, Age, Race, Class[2]

Elaine Riddick's sterilization and thousands of others came to light in an era in which norms around who ultimately should exercise control over women's fertility changed a great deal. The sterilizations struck a major chord with black female activists and other activist women of color in the midst of a major feminist push for access to abortion. One case in particular came to symbolize the problem.

In 1973, the year the women's liberation movement won an important symbolic and concrete legal victory in the Supreme Court's *Roe v. Wade* decision, news surfaced that 12-year-old Minnie Lee Relf and her 14-year-old sister Mary Alice—daughters of black Alabama farm hands—had been sterilized without consent in a federally funded clinic. Dorothy Roberts writes:

> Fourteen-year-old Minnie Lee Relf and her twelve-year-old sister Mary Alice Relf were the youngest of six children of a Black couple living in Montgomery, Alabama. The Relf parents were uneducated farmhands, who survived after migrating to the city on relief payments totaling $156 a month. In June 1973, nurses from the federally funded Montgomery Community Action Agency asked the Relfs for permission to admit the youngest Relf sisters to a hospital for injections of the long-acting experimental contraceptive Depo-Provera. Mrs. Relf, unable to read or write, signed the consent form with an "X." Apparently believing that their race and poverty made these young girls candidates for birth control, the nurse had been giving them regular shots. But that spring Washington had ordered an end to the hormonal injections when they were linked to cancer in laboratory animals. Instead, the Relfs later learned, their daughters were sterilized.[3]

Such sterilizations had been performed routinely since Southern states opened "maternity clinics" with the explicit aim of lowering the black birth rate in the 1930s. One imagines those responsible were not unaware of the sinister irony of the clinics' names. Southern doctors also frequently rendered black women infertile during other procedures. So useless was the black uterus in both the doctors' and the wider community's opinion that this came to be known as a "Mississippi appendectomy."[4]

The Relf sterilization became a symbol of the country's racially stratified system of reproductive health. At a time when women's ability to control their fertility moved from the margins to the center of the struggle for women's rights, the Relf sisters' violation was a clear reminder that the very patriarchal control of reproduction that the period's feminist activists decried had diverged sharply along racial lines historically.[5] Men indeed held far too much power regarding women's fertility, but prominent among the decisions they controlled were whose reproductive capacities were enabled and enhanced and whose were disabled and diminished.

While the Relf case brought significant attention to the problem—it became a "sensation" in the press—the Student Nonviolent Coordinating Committee (SNCC) can be credited with politicizing the problem of sterilization among blacks in the years before. SNCC members called attention to the problem of sterilization abuse as early as 1964, in their pamphlet "Genocide in Mississippi."[6]

The mounting evidence of these efforts to curtail black fertility—75,000 sterilizations in all and thus one-half of all women sterilized in federally funded clinics—convinced many women active in the Civil Rights, Black Power, and Women's movements that they must organize around the issue of race and reproduction.[7] Their upset was justified, as in 1970 black women were sterilized at twice the rate of white women and their greater dependence on public assistance made them much more vulnerable to the practice.[8]

The phenomenon that came to be known as "sterilization abuse" was arguably the catalyst for the black women's movement that arose at the end of the classical phase of the modern Civil Rights Movement, that is, 1954–1965.[9] Frances Beal (a SNCC member and founder of SNCC's Black Women's Liberation Committee), and Margaret Sloan, founder of the National Black Feminist Organization, for example, both attributed their nascent feminist consciousness to the practice.[10] The organization Beal went on to found—first the Black Women's and later the Third World Women's Alliance—would in time articulate a position on race and reproduction among black activists that confronted the specter of genocide—that is, the genocidal aspects of coercive sterilization—without categorically denying black women's need for reproductive control.

Beal was understandably outraged by the practice and argued that "perhaps the most outlandish act of oppression in modern times is the current campaign to promote sterilization of nonwhite women in an attempt to maintain the population and power imbalance between the white haves and the non-white have nots." She was aware that other women were sterilized and acknowledged this. Indeed, many Native, Puerto Rican, Chicana, and even poor white women also suffered the same fate.[11] For example, North Carolina's infamous Eugenics Board at first targeted low-income whites, though the board's victims became predominantly black as the decades wore on.[12]

But women of color in particular spoke out and organized against the practice. In fact, one of the first actions of the Women of All Red Nations (WARN) convened women from thirty Native nations in Rapid City, South Dakota to address issues including sterilization abuse.[13] Norma Jean Serena, a woman of Creek-Shawnee ancestry, brought the first legal challenges to sterilization abuse among Native women in 1973.[14] Additionally, eleven women of Mexican origin filed a civil suit against the Los Angeles County Medical center, stating that they had been forcibly sterilized between 1971 and 1974;[15] the women themselves were part of a much larger group of Latinas mobilized to end the practice. In Los Angeles and New York they came together against the practice. In 1974 Dr. Helen Rodriguez-Trias, Maritza Arrastia, editor of *Claridad*, and Dr. Raymond Rakow led the efforts to form the Committee to End Sterilization Abuse.[16]

Beal herself was particularly adept at making crosscultural and transnational connections regarding women's oppression and she did not fail to make such connections regarding sterilization abuse. Yet in her seminal article, "Double Jeopardy: To Be Black and Female," although she discussed coercive sterilization around the world, she came back to Mississippi:

> It has recently come to our attention that a massive campaign for so-called "birth control" is presently being promoted not only in the underdeveloped non-white areas of the world, but also in black communities here in the United States.... These so called "Maternity Clinics" specifically outfitted to purge black women or men of their reproductive possibilities, are appearing more and

more in hospitals and clinics across the country.... Mississippi and some of the other Southern states are notorious for this act. Black women are often afraid to permit any kind of necessary surgery because they know from bitter experience that they are more likely than not to come out of the hospital without their insides.[17]

Sterilization abuse proved particularly haunting for black women because—as singularly horrific as events like the Relf tragedy were—activists seemed most taken aback by the sterilizations' odd familiarity. They were struck by how easily they fit within a set of critical events within black women's sexual, reproductive, and caretaking history in America—a history that, as Jael Silliman states, was "shaped by coercion, cruelty and brutality."[18] Many black feminist activists drew a direct connection between sterilization abuse and coerced reproduction and enforced child neglect in the period of enslavement, where now "[i]n a perverse reversal of the role black women were forced to play during antebellum slavery—that of breeders valued primarily for their ability to produce slave children—black women's health and well-being once again became linked to their reproductive functioning, or, in this case, lack of it."[19]

The activism of black women and other women of color in response to sterilization abuse was not without influence. The activists' efforts are the reason we refer to a "reproductive-rights" and not simply an "abortion rights" movement, for example. Jennifer Nelson writes:

Women of color pushed for a more complex reproductive rights discourse: one that acknowledged that different women had varying reproductive experiences, in part, depending on their race and class position.... Women of color and poor women told a different story about the lack of reproductive control in the pre–*Roe v. Wade* period. While women of color and poor women lacked access to abortion and contraception, they also encountered reproductive abuses such as forced or coerced sterilization.[20]

Nelson states regarding black women specifically that "throughout the first half of the 1970s, black women organized to address their unique reproductive rights demands. In so doing, they contributed to the creation of a new inclusive movement for reproductive freedom."[21] For example, black women's groups joined the Relfs and the Southern Poverty Law Center in filing suit, and in 1977 the *Relf v. Weinberger* decision marked a watershed moment in black women's struggles against the forms of reproductive control to which they had long been subject in America.

In fact, not only have reproductive rights activists and organizations begun to grapple with events like the Relf sterilization—with the place of such events within African American women's history and with the meaning and consequences of this history as a whole—but so have historians and legal scholars. Political theorists, however, have yet to do so.[22] This is a critical omission, as what the *Relf* case itself symbolizes is monumental. If *Roe* remains the enduring symbol of the relationship between the control of reproduction and justice for American women, *Relf* symbolizes what that relationship has come to be for black women.

The activists most politicized by sterilization abuse—those so haunted by the phenomenon's familiarity—often reflected on what Toni Morrison refers to as the "different history" of black women.[23] It was to this different history—to the forms of use and control to which the black female body had been subject—that they turned most decisively and effectively for inspiration as they organized against the practice, and also as they challenged the white radical feminists' understanding of reproductive and gender-based oppression that was then gaining considerable traction within the mainstream women's movement. Such a turn will serve political theorists as well. *Intimate Justice* therefore charts the long and still incomplete struggle for freedom and equality for the embodied black female subject, the struggle to use the powers and capacities of the black female body freely and equally—a struggle marked by infanticides, widespread and systematic sexual violence as a weapon of racial terror, coerced sterilizations, and other racially targeted techniques of population control,[24] as well as racially biased child removal policies.[25] It then considers what insights black women's as yet complete journey, as well as the discourse the women produced in the course of this struggle, may hold for political theory. Ultimately it considers what conceptions of freedom and corrective justice are necessary for the embodied black feminine subject.

THE BLACK FEMALE BODY AND BLACK FEMINIST MOVEMENTS

American black feminist movements can be divided into three periods: the abolitionist era, the long civil rights era, and the era of retrenchment, the last of which includes the post–civil rights era and what Richard Iton has dubbed the post–post civil rights era.[26] The periods of black feminist activism evince each phase's strong ties to broader struggles against racial domination, yet each movement also remained in dialogue with contemporaneous women's movements.[27] The first period includes women active in formal abolitionist organizations and those who resisted the institution of slavery from within—including Harriet Jacobs and Margaret Garner. As Ula Taylor states, these abolitionist feminists "organized simultaneously against slavery as a legal institution and against racially gendered sexual oppression."[28] The early phase of the long second period—from the Emancipation Proclamation through *Plessy v. Ferguson*, the *Voting Rights Act*, and *Roe v. Wade* to *Relf v. Weinberger*—includes women active in the "nadir"-era struggles for the right to vote, for an end to black economic and labor subordination, and against racial violence. Women active in this period include the liberal-leaning Anna Julia Cooper and the more radical Ida B. Wells. These black female activists supported suffrage, even when white suffragists did not support them. As well, they challenged the failure of women's organizations of the period to recognize the problem of racial violence.

Activists in the latter part of the long second period include women who left classical-phase civil-rights organizations as well as mainstream second-wave feminist organizations to form such organizations as the Third World Women's Alliance, the Combahee River Collective, the National Welfare Rights Organization, and to a lesser extent the National Black Feminist Organization.[29] The third period was characterized by greater "professionalization and institutionalization," as many active in this era were members of the academy.[30]

Iris Marion Young states that all people who are oppressed "suffer some inhibition of their ability to develop and exercise their capacities and express their needs."[31] One of the most significant and enduring insights of black feminist thought—most powerfully and succinctly stated by the members of the Combahee River Collective—is that race-, class-, and gender-based oppressions are inextricably bound together, "interlocking."[32] Wary and then simply weary of claims that the conditions under which black women lived, labored, and loved would improve after the women put in time liberating groups that could only partially account for their experience as blacks, as women, and as workers, the members of the Combahee River Collective went on to claim that black women's liberation was not adjunct to anyone else's, not black men's, not the workers of the world, and not white women's. One important aspect of this interlocking oppression to which black feminist writing and activism consistently returns is the longstanding inhibition of black women's intimate—that is sexual, reproductive, and caretaking—capacities under successive systems of racial domination.

In order to place black women's activism and their claims regarding their inhibited intimate capacities in context it is important to note that labor historian Jacqueline Jones states that black women have occupied two seemingly ironic positions throughout American history.[33] First, they were expected to perform exploitative productive labor typically reserved for those who possessed masculine embodiment, an expectation that diverged significantly from dominant conceptions of "women's work." Angela Davis notes that this made black women "anomalies." Second, they were considered suitable for a form of marginal, often backbreaking, and always exploitative women's work—work within the white intimate sphere, and work that served to meet the bodily needs of white families often at the expense of care for the bodily needs of their own. In light of the nauseating romantic notions that surround this occupation in particular, note that Phyllis Palmer found evidence that mistresses and servants came to consensus on the least desirable tasks—including pre-mechanized laundering, washing dishes, and taking care of children on evenings and weekends—and that black domestics went on to perform these tasks. Thus, though black women performed "women's work" in white homes, it was the most universally despised aspects of that work and functioned to diminish their expansive use of the powers and capacities of the female body for themselves and their families.[34]

The women were coerced into performing the labors outlined above by force within the period of enslavement and then under severe economic duress coupled with the threat of violence after Emancipation.[35] After Emancipation they were shut out from all other labor positions through violence and white female worker hate strikes, that is, when white women went on strike not for better wages and conditions but to protest black women joining the white labor force.[36]

Black feminists across generations maintained that both forms of black women's work—exploitative agricultural and industrial labor as well as marginal, menial, thankless, and very often invisible labor within white households that kept them out of their own homes— were unjust and indeed dehumanizing, not least of all because they denied women the time and ability to love and provide care for their families.

Scholars of black women's history agree that the development of "a distinctly feminist consciousness" among black women began during the period of enslavement.[37] Frederick Douglass's claim that a slave must free his mind aside, slavery was first and foremost a system of control and use of the black body; and the aforementioned distinctive consciousness is evident in the women's patterns of resistance against the racist patriarchal body politics of slavery and in their discursive output. For example, the historical record reveals that enslaved women devoted considerable attention to liberation from constraints on their bodies, which limited their ability to make choices regarding whether or not to engage in sexual relations, to reproduce, and to provide care. Notably—given the agricultural labor the women performed—there was no cultural expectation that women fashion their bodies as objects of the male gaze, nor an expectation that they exhibit typically feminine characteristics like a lack of bodily strength. However, they were expected to relinquish the most feminine capacities of their bodies to the use and control of white men, to make the most intimate capacities of their bodies available to slave masters and in truth, with regard to sexual relations, to all men.

They were compelled to provide sexual services, they were forced to reproduce, and they were forced to provide care, often wholly inadequate, to enslaved dependents and to provide far better resourced care to white children. The women, however, resisted this use and control of the female body within the system. They are credited with originating the struggle against sexual harassment in the American workplace, and their bravery in this regard would be repeated several generations later by the black women who brought the first legal challenges to workplace sexual harassment in the twentieth century.[38] The women also rarely attempted to escape enslavement without their children and, when familial escape was not an option, often chose truancy, or short-term absences, over running away in order to exert as much power as they could in rearing their children.[39] Escape remained a form of resistance most often undertaken by enslaved men.[40]

Many early women's-rights activists had been a part of the aforementioned abolitionist movement. As white female activists shifted from fighting to end slavery to fighting for woman's equal rights they often came into conflict with female members of the black equal-rights movement. The mainstream women's movement's black female contemporaries, including the clubwomen Cooper, Wells, and Mary Church Terrell, supported women's suffrage but criticized white feminists for failing to address the problem of pervasive racial violence—that is, violence against the body of the black subject—in

the period. Wells and Terrell fought and organized for an immediate
end to racial violence, violence that included lynching and, as Cooper
reminded black male activists, widespread sexual violence against
black women as well as direct assaults on independent black households, the realm in which the physical and emotional needs of the
black body were met. The root cause of the violence was the belief
that the black body existed to serve whites and that the black female
body, in particular, existed to meet the physical, emotional, and
sexual needs of the white body, although whites employed different
means to compel this than in the period of enslavement.

Wells holds the distinction of first establishing the connection
between white antiblack violence and black economic and political
subordination in the nadir of American race relations.[41] She also
named the racialized gender politics at work in the ideology that justified lynching, where the practice ostensibly served to protect chaste
white womanhood and not white male political status and economic
interests. Wells boldly stated that not all white women were chaste
and that not all black women lacked virtue. Terrell and Cooper joined
Wells in her tireless anti-lynching advocacy. Cooper went one step
further, however: she centered the body of the black female subject
as an object of racial violence in her work and famously held that
there could be no celebration of black advancement at all in a world
that condoned the sexual violation of black women. Each woman was
a member of the National Association of Colored Women, an organization that came into being to challenge the widespread belief that
black women could not be victims of sexual violence because they
were incapable of refusing demands for sex—that they were always
willing. The organization institutionalized black women's struggles
throughout the nation for an end to pervasive violence against the
black female body, and with it the cultural expectation that the black
female body existed, as it had in slavery, for the emotional, physical,
and sexual service of the needs of the white body.[42]

The clubwomen have been criticized—rightly—for the tyranny of
their "politics of respectability," which held that properly restrained
black female sexual behavior would help to secure black women's

bodies, that black women's behavior in the sphere of intimate relations could help to end racist sexual violence.[43] Middle-class members, as well as members who aspired to the middle class and thus
shared their values, often attempted to restrain the sexual, domestic, and leisure behavior of lower-class women. Lower-class women
did not simply acquiesce to this. Happily, there existed a concurrent
popular counter-discourse regarding black female sexual behavior in
this time of rampant sexual violence against black women and with
it a more expansive vision of black female intimate life, one which,
I will argue, corrective racial-justice theorists should heed and seek
to instantiate in the present.

Angela Davis and Daphne Duval Harrison include blues women
who rejected the aforementioned women's attempts to regulate
lower-class women's sexual and leisure behavior among the ranks of
the period's black feminists. Ma Rainey and Bessie Smith, for example, produced their own brand of feminist consciousness and models
of "an assertive, independent and sexually aware" black woman.[44]
Thus female blues singers offered an alternate vision of black female
sexual life, diminished but unbroken violence. Most notably, the
black feminist blues tradition included models of autonomous, sexually aware black womanhood. The tradition did not thematize motherhood and celebrated undomesticated and even non-heterosexually
oriented black female sexuality. Black women's resistance to violent
white supremacist campaigns after the period of enslavement, then,
took a variety of forms.

Recall that throughout this second period of black women's activism, in addition to the rampant racial and racialized sexual violence, black women remained largely confined to agricultural and
domestic labor in white homes, both forms of employment poorly
paid and necessitating long hours. The few black women who worked
in industrial sectors were confined to the most menial, poorly paid,
and dirtiest positions. All forms of work often prevented the women
from providing adequate care to their families. They lived within a
cultural and political context that, in addition to refusing to protect
them from sexual assault, encouraged and at times compelled them

to perform productive labor and discouraged meeting the needs of black partners and dependents—at times, as we will see, through violence.

The black women who came to feminist consciousness at the end of the classical phase of the Civil Rights Movement and the Black Power movement may hold the distinction of having had the most contentious relationship with their period's mainstream women's movement. Among their major critiques of white feminists, both liberal and radical, was that the women tended to ignore all but gender-based oppression and to focus on the particular ways in which the capacities of the white female body were inhibited—as was the case with the fight for access to abortion—and then go on to claim a sisterhood born out of women's common experiences of gendered oppression that had never existed. Black feminist activists were critical of the mainstream liberal and radical second wave's view of women and work and of their body politics, including the politics of reproduction, and this critique turned on the fact that black and white women had been subject to distinct forms of capacity inhibition under patriarchy.

The period's black feminist activists would return to the historic distinctions in black female labor force participation outlined above again and again in their critiques, specifically to the iconic labor force arrangement wherein a black woman was forced to care for the physical and emotional needs of a white body at the expense of providing such care to black bodies. They would draw attention to the distinctions in use, control, and capacity inhibition in black and white bodies under patriarchy. They would also return to the theme of violence raised by Jim Crow–era feminist activists and the distinctions in the social contexts in which black and white women lived. Earlier black feminist thinkers like Jacobs and Cooper were aware of the labor that black women performed in service of white life, and they did not approve of it, to be sure, but they did not make it a central concern as did the women in this latter period. The latter activist women held that it was not simply that there was a "difference" in women's experiences with regard to sexuality, reproduction, and care across racial lines, but there was also no denying the fact that the intimate-sphere labor of one group disproportionately benefited the other throughout American history. Implicit in their critiques lay the claim that racialized labor arrangements ensured that the white body had received far more than the physical and emotional support it was due while, conversely, the black body had received far less—a justice claim, and noticeably one that is not wholly about the problematic distributive aspects of the arrangement.

The longstanding differences in the support afforded the spheres in which the bodily needs of whites and blacks were met, to which black feminists made reference, included the coerced support by which black women raised the standard of white dependent-care provision. Black women's confinement to work as domestics, cooks, nannies, and washerwomen in and for white homes—the fact that the black female body so long labored to serve the needs of the white body—thus stood as a major stumbling block on the road to sisterhood in the second wave.[45] Tera Hunter, in her study of black domestics, laundresses, and seamstresses in Atlanta after Emancipation, puts it bluntly and confirms the claims of earlier activists, stating, for example, that "white Southern domesticity at nearly every level of society was built on the backs of black women."[46] Hunter notes that a black laundress was often the first outlay within white women's discretionary income. The politics of racial subordination had thus been instrumental in creating and sustaining the very "personal" that the feminists of the second wave would seek to politicize.

The period's black feminists decried the careerist focus among the more liberal of the second wave. Their subtext—if it can be called that—was "you clearly have no idea what work is." In response to Betty Friedan's cry that "I want something more than my husband and my children and my house," bell hooks drew attention to the glaring silences in Friedan's call: "She did not discuss who would be called in to take care of the children and maintain the home if more like herself were free from their house labor and given equal access with white men to the professions."[47] And so, hooks argued, in both the things she asked for and the questions she failed to ask, Friedan "made her plight and the plight of white women like herself synonymous with a condition affecting all American women," when in truth her plight was nothing like that of "a babysitter, factory worker, clerk or prostitute."[48] The critique arose again out of longstanding differences in black and white female labor force participation, and with it distinctions in white and black female capacity inhibition.

hooks went on to claim that had black women been called on to articulate a theory of liberation, counter to the mainstream second-wave feminist view, they would not have focused on productive labor as the route to that freedom.[49] As well, "[h]ad black women voiced their views on motherhood, it would not have been named as a serious obstacle to our freedom as women." hooks goes on to say:

> Historically, black women have identified work in the context of family as humanizing labor, work that affirms their identity as women, as human beings showing love and care, the very gesture of humanity white supremacist ideology claimed black people were incapable of expressing.[50]

It was the ironic history Jones documents above, as well as the distinctions in capacities inhibited in black and white female bodies under patriarchy, that hooks had in mind when she noted the distinctions in the conceptions of liberation that existed between white feminists and black women. It should be noted that one of the black women's groups of this period actually came far closer to defining liberation in a way that spoke to the babysitters, factory workers, clerks, and prostitutes of hooks' concern. Members of the National Welfare Rights Organization, a group composed of black single mothers, expressed a different notion of women's liberation from that presented by Friedan. Premilla Nadasen states:

> Their notion of what constituted "women's liberation" was rooted in their experiences of racial and gender discrimination and class exploitation—having to work at low-paying, menial, and often dangerous employment outside the home. Thus, their

version of women's liberation included the right to stay home and raise their children as well as seek employment outside the home; access to reproductive control (not only abortion); the right to be involved in a relationship with a man if they wanted to and on their own terms.[51]

Perhaps the greatest tragedy in this is that their list of desires does not differ radically from those of Harriet Jacobs, as detailed in her slave narrative, *Incidents.*

hooks—who had the benefit of hindsight and spoke of Friedan in the measured language of utterances and silences—was far more polite than Frances Beal, who spoke in the moment. Beal called the situation Friedan described "idle dreaming"—not a bad turn of phrase to lob at a woman bored with her leisure.[52] Beal affirmed the account of women's oppression outlined by the NWRO and went on to say that "in a society where the ideal model of a woman was a conspicuous consumer, who primped and preened all day, estranged from real work and able to limit life's functions to a simple sex role," black women had never had such "phony luxuries," as most had to enter remunerative labor markets, whether they wanted to or not. Beal pulled no punches:

> Furthermore, it is idle dreaming to think of black women simply caring for their homes and children like in the middle-class white model. Black women make up a substantial percentage of the black working force and this is true for the poorest black family as well as the so-called "middle-class" family. Black women were never afforded any such phony luxuries. Though we have been browbeaten with this white image, the reality of the degrading and dehumanizing jobs that were relegated to us quickly dissipated this mirage of "womanhood."

Those critical of the dominant second-wave position, like Beal, could claim—with activist flair and yet also with little exaggeration—that materially every aspect of the white American intimate sphere had been supported by black women:

> Very few of these [white] women suffer the extreme economic exploitation that most black women are subjected to day by day. If they find housework degrading and dehumanizing, they are financially able to buy their freedom—usually by hiring a black maid.[53]

Many white women caught up in wanting something "more" than husband, house, and children failed to realize that so much of what they already had rested largely on the grossly underpaid backs of—bodies of—black women. It did not help matters that black women often provided this support under conditions of extreme physical and economic coercion, supplemented by hate strikes, and then went home to resource deprived and, often, violent communities. Beal argued that the black woman had been sexually abused—on the way to work, at work, and on the way home from work—and economically exploited, that her image was maligned, and through it all she was "forced to serve as the white woman's maid and wet nurse for white offspring while her own children were, more often than not, starving or neglected"[54]—here again we see the bodily needs of the women's partners and dependents unmet as they labored to sustain white life. And even as black women left direct service in white homes as maids, cooks, and nannies, and direct service to white homes as laundresses and seamstresses, their work in service occupations continued to make possible white women's advancements in the professions.[55]

Among the second wave's decidedly less careerist radical arm, black feminists critiqued this segment's singular focus on patriarchy as the source of women's oppression and the understanding of patriarchal body politics that accompanied this narrow understanding of women's oppression.

Radical second-wave activists, for their part, were among the first to reverse the phrase—and thus the locus of concern—from that of "the body politic" to the politics of the body. And although concerns about reproduction and the household labor necessary to sustain a family's biological life disproportionately performed by women both surfaced within the first wave of the American women's movement, these issues became central to feminist critiques of existing social arrangements in the second wave. Susan Bordo states that while Foucault is often credited with developing a political conception of the body, North American feminist activists and thinkers preceded him in understanding the body as an object of politics.[56] Among them were the activists who, in the 1960s, protested the Miss America pageant and the sexual objectification of women the pageant encouraged.

As well—and perhaps even more iconically than the misnamed "bra burners" above—Nelson quotes Susan Brownmiller as saying abortion "made" second-wave feminism. It is true that in the debates leading up to the passage of *Roe v. Wade* radical feminists successfully convinced their more career-oriented liberal counterparts that placing the ability to control reproduction into the hands of women themselves was key in ending women's oppression. At first liberal feminist activists, like those affiliated with the National Organization for Women (NOW), did not consider such "personal issues." But radical feminists argued that women would be forever subordinate to men until they possessed the ability to control their fertility:

> The [radical feminist group] Redstockings made abortion into an issue of women's autonomy in the years immediately preceding the 1973 Supreme Court decision legalizing abortion, *Roe v. Wade*. They were some of the first feminists to demonstrate that abortion concerned women's bodies and, therefore, should be controlled by women, not male doctors, lawyers, judges and legislators.[57]

The activists were able to place the body—here specifically women's ability to exercise control over the reproductive capacities of their bodies—front and center within the women's movement. In their enthusiasm to do this, however, they overreached and made an equality claim regarding the operation of patriarchal power on the female body that did not ring true to women of color. Nelson writes, "[p]art of the message offered by groups such as Redstockings was that abortion concerned all women equally." Therefore, "[t]hey maintained that every woman needed to get involved in challenging anti-abortion laws because without the fundamental right to control reproduction in every instance, women remained subject to men."[58] The claim that abortion concerned all women equally—and the narrow understanding of the way in which patriarchal power intersected with the female body to sustain women's oppression on which it was founded—would come back to haunt them.

By making access to abortion central to ending women's oppression, radical feminists not only privileged how patriarchal power intersected with the white female body to inhibit its capacities, they also obscured what that power functioned to enable and enhance in the white female body, for this power discouraged the white female body's productive labor capacities, but it also encouraged and enhanced its reproductive capacities and devoted considerable resources to ensuring that body devote itself to meeting the bodily needs of partners and dependents. They were soundly criticized for their myopia.

Abortion-rights and other radical second-wave activists may well have brought the politics of women's bodies front and center in women's-rights efforts, but black feminists had a long tradition of writing and activism around the operation of power on the black body, on the black female body. They were, then, well positioned to critique this all-too-narrow account of body politics and, as we saw above, critique they did. As well, in the struggle for fertility control, even black feminists who conceded that black women needed access to abortion drew attention to the fact that black women had very different stories to tell regarding this need. As Angela Davis writes:

> When Black and Latina women resort to abortions in such large numbers, the stories they tell are not so much about their desire

to be free of their pregnancy, but rather about the miserable social conditions which dissuade them from bringing new children into the world.[59]

Black feminists, then, spoke of how social contexts, including the disproportionate institutional and interpersonal violence in black communities, and not simply lack of abortion access constrained their ability to make choices in their intimate lives, to provide adequate care.

Like Wells, Terrell, and Cooper, who critiqued white suffragists' sole focus on the extension of formal legal rights to women while ignoring rampant violence against blacks, Audre Lorde, too, drew attention to the disproportionate violence in black women's lives. In "Man Child: A Black Lesbian Feminist's Response," she spoke of the difficulty she faced as a black woman raising a son in New York City and indeed gives an account of black feminine and black dependent bodies under threat. She called the racist environment in which she and her son resided a "suicidal dragon."[60] In "Age, Race, Class and Sex" she is less succinct but no less poetic. She speaks of black women living in the trenches and the difficulty white women and even white feminists had in relating to their experiences, because they did not live in an environment where they fought daily in "the war against dehumanization."[61]

For Lorde, one of the major barriers to black and white sisterhood was the violence "stitched" into the lives of black mothers and children as a function of the distinctive racist social environments in which they resided. A white woman had the luxury of believing, she says, that if she was "good enough, pretty enough, sweet enough, quiet enough, teach the children to hate the right people and marry the right man, then you will be able to co-exist with patriarchy in relative peace." Part of that luxury was provided by a state that opted to secure white neighborhoods—and thus white bodies—from risks in a way that it refused to do for blacks. Black women and children did not have the luxury of living with patriarchy in peace. In a world where dehumanization was "ceaseless," black women and children knew that "the fabric of our lives is stitched with violence and with hatred, that there is no rest."[62] She goes on to say:

> For us, increasingly, violence weaves through the daily tissues of our lives, in the supermarket, in the classroom, in the elevator, in the clinic and the schoolyard. From the plumber, the baker, the saleswoman the bus driver the bank teller, the waitress who does not serve us.[63]

Lorde also spoke of the unbridgeable differences between white and black feminisms as a result of this violence, and summed up the failures of sisterhood thus:

> Some problems we share as women and some we do not. You fear your children will grow up to join the patriarchy and testify against you; we fear our children will be dragged from a car and shot down in the street and you will turn your backs upon the reasons they are dying.[64]

An impassible gulf indeed.

FEMINIST POLITICAL THEORY AND THE BLACK FEMALE BODY

In light of the above, I would like to turn to what have been the considerable insights of feminist political theory and consider how best to bring them together with the insights of black feminist thought in order to develop accounts of freedom and corrective racial justice capable of addressing the legacy of racist patriarchal body politics and bodily capacity inhibition, where central to both will be addressing the disproportionate violence black women have suffered and continue to suffer. I will also consider how to bring feminist political theory and black feminist thought together to address black women's contemporary needs.

In keeping with the radical feminist slogan that "the personal is political," one of the most significant contributions of feminist political theory to the broader discipline has been the critique of the public/private divide.[65] Feminists held that the realm of sexuality, reproduction, and care was profoundly political space and were therefore critical of traditional thinkers for whom "norms of freedom, equality and reciprocity have stopped at the household door."[66] By failing to consider domestic space, the feminist thinkers held, the traditional thinkers excluded "an entire domain of human activity" from moral and political considerations, thereby deeming it a part of the realm of nature and, as Seyla Benhabib states, "beyond the pale of justice."[67]

Feminist political theorists have challenged traditional political theorists to consider the status of women, women's customary roles, and their labors and activities within the sphere of intimate relations in accounts of ideal social organization. Here and elsewhere I use the phrases "intimate sphere" and "sphere of intimate relations" to refer to one among the three realms that have been considered private in Western political thought. Benhabib notes that the term "private" refers to three distinct concepts or zones of privacy in the Western tradition. The first is the sphere of moral and religious conscience, set apart from public power in the modern era. The second refers to economic liberties. The final sense refers to the "domain of the household, of meeting the daily needs of life, of sexuality, reproduction, of care for the young, the sick and the elderly."[68] It is this third notion of privacy that concerns me here and that feminist critique most often targets.

Feminist theories of ideal social organization take into account the tasks that women disproportionately perform in the sphere of intimate relations and the effect of those tasks and activities on women's participation in other—often more socially valued—spheres of life. They hold that the sexual division of labor is a major obstacle to women's opportunities in society at large.[69] They have also claimed that there are unjust harms associated with occupying the subordinated half of a gender binary in an andro-centric society, a society that uniformly privileges traits associated with masculinity.[70]

It is an impressive body of work. Most pointedly, here I would like to consider Nancy Hirschmann's feminist revisions to mainstream conceptions of constraint and freedom, Moira Gatens's critiques of how modern thinkers "embodied" the modern state, and Iris Marion Young's oppression-centered account of injustice complete with its attentiveness to the disproportionate violence that members of op-pressed groups experience. Finally I consider Martha Nussbaum's elaboration of the ten central capabilities in conversation with in-sights of black feminist thought above in order to bring to the fore the distinctions regarding gendered capacity inhibition within the latter tradition. This is done in an effort to elaborate conceptions of freedom and corrective racial justice that can adequately ac-count for black women's historical experiences and respond to their contemporary needs.

For example, consider the aims of Young's oppression-centered account of justice, an account she advances as an alternative to what she calls "the distributive paradigm," where scholars conceive of "jus-tice and distribution as coextensive concepts."[71] She states that while "any conception of justice must address the distribution of material goods . . . many public appeals to justice do not concern primarily the distribution of material goods."[72] For Young, "[j]ustice should not only refer to distribution, but also to the institutional conditions necessary to the development and exercise of individual capacities." Young, then, wishes to "displace talk of justice that regards persons as primarily possessors and consumers of goods to a wider context that includes action, decisions about action, and provisions of the means to develop and exercise capacities."[73] I am persuaded by this more expansive conception of justice and think that an engagement with Hirschmann's work on freedom and Nussbaum's elaboration of the capabilities approach can help us to bring it about. It is important for those concerned with racial justice to remember that, beyond the maldistribution of material goods that results from blacks' being shut out from all but the most menial occupations historically, the denial of equal concern and respect to blacks created and continues to support significant group differences in relative capacity development within the intimate sphere. This conception is helpful, as well, for thinking about corrective racial justice, which under this conception would not only involve redistributing resources and positions of social advantage, but—given how black women's intimate capacities have long been diminished historically—also involve creating supportive, secure, and even regenerative contexts where black women have true freedom of action with regard to their intimate lives and where they may develop their intimate capacities. Additionally, Young names the disproportionate violence to which members of oppressed groups are subject as an important "face" of their oppression, and addressing the disproportionate violence to which black women are subject is absolutely critical to any intimate racial justice project.

While Young holds that we must be afforded the conditions necessary to develop and exercise our capacities, Martha Nussbaum provides a concrete list of which among our capacities political communities should develop and support. She lists the following ten central capabilities: life, bodily health, bodily integrity, "sense, imagination and thought," emotions, practical reason, affiliation, other species, play, and control over one's political and material environment.

I turn to Nussbaum in greater detail below. Yet before I outline my plan to bring feminist political theory and black feminist thought together I would like to turn my attention to Afro-Modern thought and the place of black feminist authors within that tradition, as *Intimate Justice* is also an intervention into "Afro-Modern" political thought. The contrast between male and female Afro-Modernists' presentation of life under key systems of racial domination will form an important part of the backdrop for my efforts. I should note, however, that Nussbaum's elaboration of the central capabilities has informed my analysis of male- and female-authored texts within Afro-Modern thought.

AFRO-MODERN POLITICAL THOUGHT AND THE BLACK BODY

Robert Gooding-Williams names "Afro-Modern" as a distinct genre of modern political thought. The genre, he says, is composed of "a rich body of argument and insight . . . bound together by certain genre-defining thematic preoccupations." It emerged in the late eighteenth century and "forged a distinct intellectual configuration." Gooding-Williams goes on to list familiar figures within the tradition, including "Otrabah Cugoano, Olaudah Equiano, Martin R. Delany and Frederick Douglass; C.L.R. James, Frantz Fanon, and Walter Rodney; Booker T. Washington, and naturally, W.E.B. Du Bois." He states that "in sharp contrast to the social contract, French liberal and most other tendencies in modern political thought, works within the Afro-Modern tradition are less concerned with the legitimate authority and properly restrained power of the nation-state and more concerned with outlining the political and social organization of successive systems of racial domination, the nature and effects of successive systems of racial ideology and the possibilities of black emancipation."[74] From Douglass and Du Bois to contemporary Afro-Modern thinkers Charles W. Mills and Tommie Shelby, the tradition's intricate treatments of black life within successive systems of racial domination—from the "New World" plantation system and the Jim Crow order to contemporary residential segregation complete with racialized uneven development—have done much to illuminate the production and maintenance of black constraint and inequality. They have also put forward impressive theoretical solutions to the problem of racial domination.

Du Bois's *The Souls of Black Folk*, for example, Gooding-Williams says, is an "exploration of how to create and conduct a politics for African-Americans that counters white supremacy in the instance of Jim Crow." He goes on to say that for Du Bois "a politics that was suitable to counter Jim Crow had to both uplift the backward black masses and to assimilate them to the constitutive norms of modernity and to heed the ethos of the black folk."[75] Problematically, for

Gooding-Williams, Du Bois understands politics as what some blacks do to and for other blacks, as a form of Weberian rule-giving with the ultimate goal of producing the expressive ethos of the black folk. He continues, "the politics of expressive self-realization proceeds through the subordination of the black masses to the directives and policy dictates of a cultured, aristocratic black leadership."[76] Douglass, however, thinks of politics as something blacks do together, through deliberation and individual initiative-taking which then encourages others to act in concert. Gooding-Williams endorses the latter vision of black politics.

Tommie Shelby and Charles Mills are also concerned with contemporary racial domination. They write in what Richard Iton has named the post–post civil-rights era, the period distinguished from the period of enslavement and Jim Crow by the extension of formal legal rights to blacks but marked instead by the inequitable application of punishments in black communities, those communities themselves being resource-deprived spaces of exception with the American body politic. Shelby and Mills share the "genre-defining thematic preoccupations" of other thinkers within the tradition as they, too, seek to elaborate the political and social organization of past and present racial domination in order to generate theoretical solutions to the problem of racial injustice.

On that which makes Afro-Modern thought modern, aside from Du Bois's explicit plan to "modernize" the black folk, the tradition responds to a set of racialized power and territorial/spatial formations that arose in the modern period—the plantation, the colony, the postcolony, and the "Dark Ghetto."

I would add that another feature that marks thinkers within the tradition as thoroughly modern is their concern for the body of the black subject and for the threats racial domination posed to that body—a concern that would strike the profoundly "somatophobic" Plato as thoroughly "womanish," as the ancient thinker understood "woman" as she who was "quintessentially body-directed" and held that to live a life overly concerned with the vile body was to act like a woman.[77] Their concern for the body fits quite comfortably, however, alongside the bodily threats and fears that ultimately drive Hobbes's natural man into civil society.[78] Like those poor harassed souls in Hobbes's state of nature, the very real fear of violent death—the specter of a life that, if not solitary, can indeed be "nasty, brutish and short"—is an ever-present concern on this, as Young reminds us, the far more violent dark side of modernity.

I will point out that male thinkers within the tradition, however, are concerned with some bodies more than others—the violence wrought against some bodies over others—*and* some capacities of the black body over others. As with social contract theory, the threats to the female body under racial domination and before the establishment of a state in the former are often raised, but fairly briefly, and then quickly brushed aside. Like their social-contract-theory antecedents who sought to free themselves in civic life but left patriarchal relationships in the private sphere largely unchanged, the most celebrate and influential works within the tradition have developed conceptions of black liberation from constraint and conceptions of racial equality that are most focused on black action in civic space, and which have correspondingly closely associated freedom and equality with particular capacities of the black body, namely the body's capacities for controlling its political and material environment.[79] The civic sphere is the privileged realm of action and therefore of insult within the texts. The realm of intimate relations and its associated capacities are either seldom mentioned, as with Douglass, or presented as lower-order concerns, as is the case with Du Bois.

In fact, if we take Nussbaum's framework as a blueprint for the ideally capable black body, male thinkers within the tradition present the black body's capacities as hierarchically ordered and go on to concentrate most pointedly on what she would call the capability of life, and on blacks' capacities for controlling their political and material environment over other capacities. Shelby, for example, uses Rawls as a guide for his theory of racial justice. Recall that Rawls's two principles of justice concern ensuring fairness in man's efforts to control his political and material environment, the two themselves lexically ranked. Nussbaum's elaboration of the central capabilities helps to shed light on the gendered bodily capacity hierarchy within the mainstream of the Afro-Modern tradition—where the body's capacities for controlling its political and material environment are held above all others and thought to be the key to freedom and corrective racial justice—that allows the capacities most closely associated with femininity to be instrumentalized in the service of the race's higher-order capacity aims, creating problems for those who possess feminine embodiment and those who would undertake the material labors associated with femininity. It helps to highlight, as well, problematic presumptions of capacity interconnection among what she holds are in fact discrete capabilities among many thinkers who would even acknowledge the impact of racial domination on black intimate capacities. This is true of Du Bois in particular—who asserts that the vote will ensure all other capacities, that if blacks are allowed to exercise their capacities for speech and action they will be afforded leave to exercise all other capacities. I turn to this in chapter 3. The thinker, however, is by no means alone in this and it is important to remain vigilant against the tendency to instrumentalize the sphere of intimate relations, the realm of sexuality and reproduction, in Afro-Modern thought and in thinking about racial justice. Neither can we assume, for example, that affording blacks' greater control over their political and material environments will afford greater protection for black bodily health and bodily integrity, and we must guard against this. Female-authored texts provide an important corrective to this capacity hierarchy, as they present a black body less hierarchically organized and less divided against itself.

And so, just as John Locke's *Second Treatise* invited immediate feminist criticism from thinkers like Mary Astell, as it announced a shift from a political world of men and women in a web of familial and sexual interconnections to a world of contractual relations among men, the most celebrated works within Afro-Modern political thought cannot, and in fact did not, escape a similar critique.[80] Yet women's writing and resistance have often been overshadowed. Therefore, in the text I contrast the work of female authors within the tradition with their male counterparts in order to develop the insights of thinkers who challenged the laser focus on masculine agency and civic space within the tradition.

CHAPTER OUTLINE

In chapter 2 I consider historical accounts of the black female experience in slavery—slave narratives authored by women as well as pioneering black feminist analysis of those narratives—alongside Nancy Hirschmann's feminist revisions to mainstream conceptions of constraint and freedom. An examination of black women's experiences in the period of enslavement reveals that women and men faced considerable constraint in exercising their capacities for forming sexual relations as well as their capacities for reproduction and caretaking. Although both sexes were constrained in this way—though women more so than men—women undertook the tragic second shift in the period of enslavement, caring for white children and providing inadequate care for children that could never truly be their own. An examination of slave narratives authored by women reveals that, unlike male-authored narratives, women focus considerable narrative attention on constraints on these capacities as opposed to others. Enslaved women were the first to outline the distinct dimensions of black women's unique constraint in the period of enslavement. Crucially, their presentations of their constraints in this period are relevant to us today because, as Dorothy Roberts states, "[Slavery] marked black women from the beginning as objects whose decisions about reproduction should be subject to social regulation rather than their own will."[81] Roberts states that the essence of black women's experience in slavery was the brutal denial of reproductive autonomy. She argues that this set the stage for the social control of black reproduction throughout American history, and she traces this social control through the early eugenic aims of the birth-control movement, the development of Norplant and Depo-Provera as tools of population management, welfare reform,[82] and even the criminalization of reproduction itself among black women with substance-abuse problems.[83] Thus enslaved women's outline of their constraints are relevant in thinking about freedom—and indeed corrective racial justice—for black women today.

Hirschmann's conception of constraint is useful as it is attentive to both agent-originated and cultural contextual barriers to women's ability to exercise their capacities freely. For Hirschmann, for example, sexism is a social force that is capable of constraining women's actions just as effectively as an individual constraining agent who intends to do so. Hirschmann's revisions also encourage us to think beyond how the slave system constrained women beyond taking away their ability to make choices—it is not simply that they have not long been able to exercise choice in sexual partners, reproduction and caretaking, but also that they have held considerably less power than whites, and particularly white men, in determining the meaning of their sexual, reproductive, and caretaking actions. Hirschmann is particularly useful in drawing the connections between the constraints black women faced in the period of enslavement and the constraints black women face today—as today's black women act and make decisions about action absent that notorious intentionally constraining agent, the slave master, absent as well Mississippi "maternity clinics," but we can certainly say that they are not free.

In chapter 3 I examine historical accounts of women's experiences within the Jim Crow Era—the high tide of blacks' disproportionate experience of violence that Young states is an important face of their oppression—as well as black feminist claims that threats to the male body in the period have overshadowed threats to the female body in the collective memory of that era. I consider parallels between black feminist critiques of accounts of Jim Crow–era violence and feminist political theorists' critiques of social-contract theory. Feminist political theorists, Moira Gatens most notably, have drawn attention to how social contract theorists "embodied" the modern state—that is, how they designed the state to protect and enhance the powers and capacities of men, of the male body. I argue that it is imperative that we be attentive to how male thinkers within the

Afro-Modern tradition would embody racial equality—which capacities of which black bodies would be most protected and enhanced under their visions of racial equality, which capacities would be instrumentalized in service of that equality, and which bodies would be simply swallowed up into the American body politic, perhaps as unprotected within it as they had been in the state of nature that was Jim Crow.

In chapter 4, I examine and critique Tommie Shelby's "Justice, Deviance and the Dark Ghetto," in particular his account of a generic and tacitly male black body's experience of racial injustice in the particular racialized territorial formation of the Dark Ghetto, as well as his use of Rawls—whose account of justice focuses on ensuring fairness in man's efforts to control his political and material environment—to evaluate past racial injustice. I suggest that, first, we remember that black men *and* women reside in "dark ghettos," and that we look to Amartya Sen and Martha Nussbaum's capability approach, as it provides a better model of how we should evaluate past and contemporary racial injustice.

That said, Shelby's application of Rawls to the problem of political obligation in black urban space is fascinating, and I respond to it with what I see as necessary feminist revisions. In "Justice, Deviance and the Dark Ghetto," Shelby argues that blacks in urban centers do not have the same set of civic obligations that bind people within the wider society. That argument is based on his claim that meaningful citizenship—defined as equal political power relative to members of the wider society, equal access to employment-oriented skill acquisition and to employment itself, equal treatment within the criminal justice system, and freedom from racially motivated police scrutiny, intimidation, harassment, and violence—does not obtain in this space. In the final section I consider how an account of racial injustice like the one Shelby presents, revised with attention to the experiences of black women, their traditional activities, the institutions that regulate social reproduction, and race- and gender-based harms in society, might change an account of political obligation within the dark ghetto.

In chapter 5, I examine Tommie Shelby's and Charles Mills's accounts of what is necessary to establish "corrective racial justice." Both thinkers look to social-contract theory in order to develop accounts of corrective racial justice, as blacks were never afforded the equality they sought after Emancipation, and now the two thinkers reflect on what justice demands beyond the extension of formal political rights and equality before the law to blacks. I argue that, by looking to social-contract theory, they embody corrective racial justice problematically, and I suggest that instead blacks look to the vision of the plurally capable body at the center of Martha Nussbaum's particular elaboration of the capabilities approach. Corrective racial justice should indeed correct, as Mills argues, for intergenerational "white opportunity hoarding" under white supremacy, but this effort should be guided by Martha Nussbaum's understanding of the body and what it requires, therefore explicitly providing redress for black women's experiences of intimate injustice—including the denial of bodily health and bodily integrity—as well as the denial of adequate support to the realm in which the physical and emotional needs of the body are met to all blacks under white supremacy.

As the sphere of intimate relations is a significant realm in which black women experience injustice, it is critical that scholars develop theories of corrective racial justice that explicitly attend to the history of racial injustice on both sides of the public/private divide and address the legacy of racialized disadvantage in the black intimate sphere. Nussbaum holds that justice requires familial polices more interventionist than Rawls would allow, and this is absolutely the case regarding corrective racial justice.

Any theory of corrective racial justice inspired by Rawls, whose theory of justice focuses on establishing fairness in man's efforts to control his political and then his material environment, must include at a minimum explicit additional provisions designed to establish justice within the black intimate sphere. It must acknowledge that our sexual, reproductive, and caretaking capacities are not natural—that they, too, require resources, protection, and support as well as social contexts in which they can be developed and exercised—and that black intimate capacities have been profoundly diminished under racial domination in ways that theories of corrective racial justice must explicitly address.

Justice requires that no one's intimate capacities be unduly constrained and that all live within contexts that support and enable equally the exercise of their intimate capacities, social contexts that provide equal opportunity to develop and exercise those capacities. Justice requires that racial-group membership must never determine whether or not one has to create intimate and caring relationships amid disproportionate violence, nor should the exercise of intimate capacities themselves expose one to interpersonal and institutional violence, as has been the case for black women throughout American history.

In closing I would like to say that while the experience of enslavement, Jim Crow, exclusion from the New Deal, residential segregation, racialized security provision, and mass incarceration—taken all together—are a set of specifically African American historical experiences, any system that allowed the longstanding exclusion of a specific group of women from state protection for women's bodily integrity and bodily health, for example, would merit intimate justice.

[2]

"WHAT FREE COULD POSSIBLY MEAN"

The Intimate Sphere in Enslaved Women's Visions of Freedom

I think now it was the shock of liberation that drew my thoughts to what "free" could possibly mean to women. In the eighties, the debate was still roiling: equal pay, equal treatment, access to professions, schools . . . and choice without stigma. To marry or not. To have children or not. Inevitably these thoughts led me to the different history of black women in this country—a history in which marriage was discouraged, impossible or illegal, in which birthing children was required, but "having" them, being responsible for them—being in other words, their parent—was as out of the question as freedom.[1]

In 1713, Arrabell would illustrate clearly and heartbreakingly the tension that was at stake for enslaved women throughout the diaspora. Arrabell lived with seven women and nine men in Berkely County. Three of the women were mothers and a fourth two-year-old child was cared for on the plantation in the absence of a named parent. The population of African slaves would shortly eclipse that of white settlers, and Arrabell and the women around her may have begun to feel portents of the changes that were about to engulf the colony. They must have watched the aftermath of many slaveowners' deaths and searched for a way to shield themselves and their children from separation and distribution among their heirs. Through the birth of their children, enslaved women may have seen a means to reappropriate what should have been theirs all along. Arrabell's child's name appears to indicate poignantly the struggle inherent in reproduction in this most unstable moment in the development of slave society. Arrabell called her child "Mines"—as she could do little else in the burgeoning slave society of South Carolina. And, of course, even as she staked this claim, she and her child were sold. The next sale may have been the one that irrevocably reminded her that Mines could not actually be hers.[2]

Procreation. That could also be a slave-breeders way of thinking . . .

No, because it depends on if it's for you or somebody else. Your life or theirs . . .
Are you mine, Ursa, or theirs?[3]

MARGARET GARNER

In 1856 Margaret Garner, her husband Robert, his parents, and Margaret's four children escaped enslavement by making a dangerous trek out of Kentucky across the frozen Ohio River. Though Ohio was a free state in the era after the ratification of the 1850 Fugitive Slave Act, crossing state lines alone did not guarantee the fugitives' safety. It may have come as little surprise to them, then, that armed bounty hunters, a posse of eleven men, cornered them in an Ohio home. Though Robert and his father shot at the posse in self-defense, it soon became apparent that the group would be taken. At that point Margaret made an extraordinary decision. Not content to see her children, particularly her daughters, returned to slavery, the mother nearly decapitated one daughter and attempted to kill a second before the posse entered the house and stilled her hand.

Garner's infanticide holds tremendous symbolic significance for all who interpret Transatlantic slavery and the statements on freedom, both verbal and non, that the system's captives produced.

Mark Reinhardt speaks of the numerous interpretations surrounding the infanticide, conflicting reports on what happened,
and the event's somewhat apocryphal status, but he notes that
those opposed to slavery, past and present, have interpreted the
infanticide as a statement on freedom: "Repeatedly, her attack on
her children was read as a blow for freedom.... She was heroic
precisely because in killing her daughter to save her from slavery
she showed she valued freedom above life itself."[4] The act certainly
secured Garner's place as a founding hero of what Paul Gilroy calls
the "black feminist political project."[5] Gilroy notes that while the
event is most certainly part of the broader slave discourse on freedom, it has been particularly important for black women writing
on slavery.

Gilroy is correct; black feminists indeed have understood the infanticide as signaling something important about enslaved women's
unique oppression and subsequent resistance efforts. Today Garner's
story is perhaps best known as the inspiration for Toni Morrison's
novel *Beloved*. Yet over a hundred years before Morrison picked up
her pen the abolitionist feminist Frances Harper, a great among early
black women writers, wrote a poem in honor of Garner entitled "The
Slave Mother: A Tale of Ohio."[6] Harper also references the infanticide as a symbol of black discontent with the institution of slavery in
her novel *Iola Leroy*, one of the first novels—long thought to be the
first novel—published by an African American woman.[7] The event is
presented as evidence of blacks' yearning to be free and serves as an
important lesson in the developing racial consciousness of the main
character, Iola.[8]

Angela Davis, in her classic article "Reflections on the Black
Woman's Role in the Community of Slaves"[9]—where she presents
the three similarities and one significant difference in the male
and female experience in slavery, that is productive labor requirements, consciousness of oppression, resistance, and systematic
sexual assault, respectively—references Garner as evidence of
both women's unique desperation and their participation in slave
resistance.[10]

In his own consideration of the infanticide Gilroy raises an interesting question, one that he himself does not answer, regarding the divergent male and female violence in response to the pursuing mob. He asks:

> What are we to make of these contrasting forms of violence, one coded as male and outward, directed towards the oppressor and the other, coded as female, somehow internal, channeled towards a parent's most precious and intimate objects of love, pride and desire?[11]

Much is made of Robert's response, of his form of resistance, both within Afro-Modern political thought and within mainstream freedom discourse. His violent, physical confrontation with white oppressors, with discrete oppressive forces wholly separate from himself and with identifiable agents of oppression—at last returning the violence that characterized whites' dealings with black men and the black male body in the period in an effort to either set black/white civic relations right or end them once and for all—conforms to the prototype of black liberation from constraint that Frederick Douglass establishes within the Afro-Modern tradition.[12] Recall that "[o]nly by overpowering his overseer was [Douglass] able to become a man—thus free—again."[13] Therefore, as Claudia Tate writes, "We unconditionally and emphatically have regarded such violent confrontations as heroic and political."[14] So, too, his violence conforms to an understanding of liberation from constraint introduced by Thomas Hobbes and perhaps best presented by Isaiah Berlin.[15] We therefore recognize such action as a decisive step toward freedom. Robert confronts discrete, identifiable, and directly constraining agents and his action is therefore straightforward, laudable. The violence is uncomplicated, simply reciprocal. There is no love lost.

Unfortunately freedom theorists are most likely to bring their interpretive powers to bear only on violence that is "coded as male." This chapter presents a response to the second compelling half of Gilroy's question: What are we to make of the violence "coded as female" and the relationship of Margaret's act to black liberation from enslavement and, importantly, to black freedom today?

In order to know what to make of the infanticide, in fact to understand it as both a pivotal act of resistance within the black feminist political project and an event worthy of consideration within contemporary freedom debates, we must take note of the constraints Margaret faced, those constraints brought about by the particular forms of use and control to which the black female body was subject within the slave system. Historians have uncovered much about Garner's life leading up to the infanticide, and this, alongside historians' accounts of the female experience in slavery, reveals much about the contours of her constraints. From these sources we know Garner lived under a system of coerced productive labor and a system that sought total control over her sexual relations as well as her reproductive and caretaking capacities, the dual system of labor and control shot through with both physical and sexual violence.[16] The sexual, reproductive, and caretaking coercion and exploitation within the slave system was a burden that fell almost exclusively on enslaved women, for as Barbara Bush-Slimani says, "power over women was exercised through control of their sexuality . . . a form of oppression rarely experienced to the same degree by enslaved men."[17] I would add that the historical record reveals that whites exercised considerable power over enslaved women's capacities for reproduction, nurture, and care in a manner not typically experienced by black men, as Deborah Gray White has noted: "Much of [the female experience in slavery] was concerned with bearing, nourishing, and rearing children whom slaveholders needed for the continual replenishment of their labor force."[18] Here, then, is the tragic second shift on the dark side of modernity.

Deborah Gray White, Barbara Bush-Slimani, and Jennifer Morgan are three among a small number of historians who have written book-length accounts of the female experience in slavery.[19] Their work supports Davis's claim that the productive labor requirements of men and women were roughly the same—that is, that the male and female body were subject to similar productive labor use and control—and her claim that the point at which the male and female experience diverged was in the sphere of intimate relations. Or, as abolitionist and author Harriet Jacobs lamented, "Superadded to the burden common to all, [women] have wrongs, and sufferings, and mortifications peculiarly their own."[20] Therefore, while Davis argues that the similarities in productive labor oppression gave rise to laudable equality in men's and women's relationships with one another in enslaved domestic space, such as it was, the control the system exercised over the sexual, reproductive, and caretaking capacities of the black female body created divergent experiences for men and women within the system. Davis states:

> But women suffered in different ways as well, for they were victims of sexual abuse and other barbarous mistreatment that could only be inflicted on women. Expediency governed the slaveholder's posture toward female slaves: when it was profitable to exploit them as if they were men, they were regarded, in effect, as genderless, but when they could be exploited, punished and repressed in ways suited only for women, they were locked into their exclusively female roles.[21]

The women were subject to systematic sexual violence and the law sanctioned black female sexual exploitation "by allowing white (and black) men to commit these assaults with impunity."[22]

Additionally, planters saw the black female body as *the* fertile body among the bodies of the enslaved and therefore as the proper target of their program of reproductive control, use, and appropriation. Morgan's extensive examination of slaveholders' wills reveals that planters considered the reproductive capacities of the enslaved woman's body in particular as an important part of what they were purchasing or selling in any transaction involving female slaves, and therefore the reproductive capacities of the enslaved female body were an express part of their speculative investment in that body. The planters' understanding of the black female body as the locus of the reproductive capacities of the enslaved had considerable impact on women's daily experiences, as planters and overseers often manipulated female sexual relations to better harness the women's reproductive capacities. Morgan writes:

> In 1737, an observer in North Carolina suggested that planters were quite mindful of enslaved women's reproductive value, writing that "a fruitful woman amongst them [is] very much valued by the planters, and a numerous issue esteemed the greatest riches in this country." He went on to suggest that slave owners interfered in the lives of enslaved couples by obliging a woman to take a "second, third, fourth, fifth and more husbands or bedfellows" if children did not appear after a "year or two." It is important to note that the manipulation of fertility here, as elsewhere, was perceived to be located in the body of the fruitful or fruitless woman, whose multiple husbands bore no reproductive responsibility.[23]

Morgan goes on to note that variations in region, crops, and household size all created diverse experiences for captives, but the experience of reproduction and conflicts between planters and black women over expectations surrounding the meaning of reproduction—what it was exactly that the woman produced when she gave birth, the meaning of the being that she produced—tended to unify enslaved women's experience as a whole.[24]

Enslaved women were also subject to other violations of their bodily integrity that ultimately served white interests as well. The torturous surgeries of J. Marlon Sims are iconic cases in point. Sims purchased female slaves for his surgical research and performed unanesthetized surgeries on their sexual and reproductive organs. Harriet A. Washington reflects on Robert Thom's painting, *J. Marlon Sims: Gynecologic Surgeon*. The painting depicts Sims performing experimental surgery on a woman he owned, Betsey. The painting presents an "innocuous tableau" that obscures "the gruesome reality in which each surgical scene was a violent struggle between the slaves and physicians and each woman's body was a bloodied battleground."[25] Washington states that in truth, "[e]ach naked, un-anesthetized slave woman had to be forcibly restrained by the other physicians through her shrieks of agony as Sims sliced, then sutured her genitalia."[26]

Slave narratives authored by women also provide guidance regarding what to make of the female coded violence as they, alongside historical accounts of female enslavement and female resistance patterns, shed light on the relative significance enslaved women attributed to their ability to live lives free of intimate constraint compared to the other constraints they faced within the system. Jacobs, for example, focuses the bulk of her narrative's attention on the constraints the system placed on her ability to make choices regarding sexual relations, reproduction, and child care; at one point in the narrative she even states that she would endure a lifetime of bonded productive labor to be free from intimate bondage.

Women authored only around 12 percent of extant slave narratives and in 1987 Mary Helen Washington lamented that "none of these is as well known as the narratives by men."[27] Washington went on to say that "[t]he result of this has been that the life of the male slave has come to be representative, even though the female experience in slavery was sometimes radically different."[28] While black feminist scholars have made strides in bringing attention to texts authored by women, the dearth of female-authored texts combined with their lesser renown means that constraint within enslavement and subsequent liberation from that constraint has come to be associated with the powers and capacities—as well as the desires and needs of and most significant threats to—the body of the male slave.

Feminists have not only challenged the representativeness of the male experience within these narratives but also how women are represented in male-authored texts. For example, women are not major characters, as "[i]n male narratives, women play subordinate roles. Men leave them behind when they escape to the North, or they are pitiable subjects of brutal treatment or benign nurturers who help the fugitive in his quest for freedom, or objects of sentimentality."[29] I would add that in the male-authored narratives the enslaved female subject is presented as being in some sense trapped by her body—trapped in her body. The female body itself invites sexual abuse, from which there are presented no avenues of redemption in a way that is not true of female body presentation in female-authored texts. Heroic reciprocal physical violence against the white male body redeems the body of the black male subject. Douglass narrates his own reciprocal violence as a resurrection—it restores his dignity and heals his wounded flesh. The texts present no reciprocal action capable of redeeming the sexually assaulted female subject. Her body's unredeemed and unredeemable status is brought home by the fact that she remains enslaved at the close of male-authored texts. As Jenny Franchot says of Douglass, "one knows women in slavery and men in freedom."[30]

Below I consider the narrative of the abolitionist Harriet Jacobs at length.[31] Carby says of Jacobs's narrative, "*Incidents in the Life of a Slave Girl* is the most sophisticated, sustained narrative dissection of the conventions of true womanhood by a black author before emancipation."[32] Washington says, "Twenty years after her escape from slavery, Harriet Jacobs published what may well be the only slave narrative that deals primarily with the sexual exploitation of slave women."[33] Her narrative is worthy of sustained consideration regarding "what free could possibly mean" to enslaved women as compared to enslaved men, because she relates the story of her constraint within the slave system as a tale of how her slaveholder restricted her ability to make choices regarding sexual relations, reproduction, and care. In fact, if we map Douglass's and Jacobs's accounts of liberation to the body itself, Douglass focuses on liberation for the work of the black hands and the black body's capacities for speech and action in addition to liberation from physical violence, while Jacobs's narrative focus concerns liberating the labor of the black body—that is, the capacities of the body and the material labors that have come to define the feminine—as well as liberating that body from sexual and reproductive violence. Consideration of Douglass's narrative alone in thinking about what free could possibly mean would certainly leave the black female body in particular half-slave, half-free.

However, as important as it is, her narrative can only take us so far regarding what free could possibly mean for women. In our consideration of female coded violence, it is important as well to think about other aspects of enslaved women's intimate constraint than those on display in Jacobs. This is the case because, although Jacobs's narrative crucially shifts the focus regarding black liberation to distinct capacities of the body, like Douglass's it focuses on discrete agents of constraint—Covey for Douglass, Flint for Jacobs—and does not address that which is "somehow internal."[34] Both authors also tell the story of a fully formed, self-seeking liberation, although for Jacobs, as Smith points out, it is a self-in-relationship. This self comes to understand his or her constraints and that which he or she desires and makes a plan for freeing himself or herself from said constraints in order to realize what he or she desires. Therefore, finally I want to argue that, in order to fully understand female coded violence, we must finally turn to the feminist freedom theorist Nancy Hirschmann.

The historical record reveals that forms of use and control of the enslaved female body to which Garner's infanticide responds, female-authored narratives, coupled with the record of women's intimate-sphere resistance efforts, help to shed light on the significance women attributed to these constraints relative to other constraints they faced. Hirschmann can help us move from consideration of the external forces constraining black women's intimate capacities to internal ones, as well as to reflect on significant issues of meaning creation within the system. Both of these forms of constraint are crucial in thinking about the connections between Garner's constraints and those facing black women today in contexts that lack slave masters, sterilizing doctors, and other agents of population control. Through consideration of Hirschmann's feminist account of freedom we see that black women's constraints within enslavement involved much more than an external agent restricting their ability to make choices regarding their intimate lives, and she helps us to see how many of these other constraints persist in the present. Hirschmann helps to explain why Garner could provide inspiration for Morrison so many years later, as Morrison sensed that black women were in some important sense still not free even though there were no slave masters to be found. Hirschmann can help us to think about women's intimate constraints within the slave system, and black women's intimate constraints today, as involving much more than external agents preventing them from making choices regarding sexuality, reproduction, and caretaking such as are highlighted in the Jacobs narrative. She moves us toward an understanding of unfreedom that includes constrained meaning creation and the constraints of a racist and sexist social context that shapes that which is "somehow internal."[35] What this means is that if we construct an account of black liberation taking Douglass alone as a guide, the black female body will certainly remain half-slave, half-free, but if we construct it only with the addition of Jacobs, which would importantly have us seek to remove constraints on intimate capacities on equal terms with removing constraints on the black body's capacities for speech and action, we might be tempted to endeavor to remove only external constraints on black women's intimate capacities without addressing the internal and nor the ways in which this internal is shaped by constraining racist sexist social contexts. If we bring Hirschmann to bear on thinking about enslaved women's constraints we get a more complete picture of all that they faced, and greater clarity regarding black women's constraints today. Hirschmann's work, then, stands as a complement to Saidiya Hartmann's account of the post-Emancipation transformation of white power over the black body as she directs our attention to such important issues as the formation of desire in patriarchal cultural contexts, and therefore to constraints that have long survived the demise of the slave master, and that we must address today.

Saidiya Hartman gives a powerful account of one important transformation in white power over the black body post-Emancipation. She says:

> The absolute dominion of the master, predicated on the annexation of the captive body and its standing as the "sign and

surrogate" of the master's body, yielded to an economy of bodies, yoked and harnessed, through the exercise of autonomy, self-interest, and consent. The use, regulation, and management of the body no longer necessitated its literal ownership since self-possession effectively yielded modern forms of bonded labor.... Although no longer the extension and instrument of the master's absolute right or dominion, the laboring black body remained a medium of others' power and representation. If the control of the black body was formerly effected by absolute rights of property in the black body, dishonor, and the quotidian routine of violence, these techniques were supplanted by the liberty of contract that spawned debt-peonage, the bestowal of right that engendered indebtedness and obligation and licensed naked forms of domination and coercion, and the cultivation of a work ethic that promoted self-discipline and induced internal forms of policing. Spectacular displays of white terror and violence supplemented these techniques.[36]

Hartman provides an account of how the black body continued to be constrained and controlled even without the direct and overt constraints of the slave master. Though the constraints of discipline and contract are important, they do not make up the totality of black women's constraint today. I argue that this understanding of white power over the black body must be supplemented with consideration of how whites retained power by retaining control over meaning creation and the social contexts that shaped and continue to shape black women's desires and wills.

That said, Hirschmann does not do enough to confront the internal. I would go further, and I turn to this in the final section. She does not go far enough regarding something that Jacobs's narrative, as a dissection of the cult of true womanhood, makes abundantly clear: that the black and white worlds are different, that the contexts in which black women and white women are forced to make choices are completely different. This all-important patriarchal cultural context which structures women's choices and desires are vastly different.

Finally, in light of "the help" that Hirschmann ultimately holds that women need in order to be free, I turn to Gatens in the next chapter, to talk about the fact that not only did black women not get help, they were often greeted with harm.

There is, then, much to consider as we reflect on what we should make of the infanticide. Douglass looms very large in the black liberation struggle. Perhaps it is only fitting that I turn to him now.

DE-CENTERING THE MASCULINE BODY OF THE REPRESENTATIVE ENSLAVED POLITICAL ANIMAL

Among texts within the slave narrative genre, narratives penned in the "middle period" are the focus of most scholarly attention.[37] The middle-period narratives were abolitionist tracts written with the express purpose of presenting slavery's most inhumane aspects in an effort to turn whites against the institution. The best-known work within this subgenre is *Narrative of the Life of Frederick Douglass, an American Slave.* This middle-period narrative has become the standard tale of black liberation and more. Wilson Jeremiah Moses says that the "1845 *Narrative*'s belated attainment of canonical status in American letters is symbolized by its inclusion in recent editions of the *Norton Anthology of American Literature*, where it is introduced with the interesting assertion that Douglass's life "has become the heroic paradigm for all oppressed people."[38] A towering figure indeed.

The outsized place of Douglass's story among all narratives is perhaps understandable. His rise from slavery to freedom was quite remarkable. Born in 1818, he escaped slavery in 1838 and by 1840, he "was well on his way to establishing himself as the principal black abolitionist in the United States."[39] A true "American Hero," whom Moses likens to Abraham Lincoln, P.T. Barnum, and Ralph Waldo Emerson, Douglass belongs in the pantheon of the quintessentially American "self-made" men.[40]

Moses states that Douglass's status as representative is open to several challenges, however.[41] He cannot be said, for example, to represent ethnocentric nationalists like Martin Delany and Alexander Crummell.[42] Moses also notes feminist criticism of Douglass's canonical status.[43] Those scholars have critiqued the fact that Douglass's narrative does little to challenge the myth of American manhood. Smith writes, "His broad-based indictments notwithstanding, by telling the story of one man's rise from slavery to the station of esteemed orator, writer, and statesman, he confirms the myth shared by generations of American men that inner resources alone can lead to success." She goes on to say, "His struggle for survival requires him to overcome numerous obstacles, but through his own talents (and some providential assistance) he finds the Promised Land of a responsible social position, a job, and a wife."[44]

Given its status as the "master narrative" of black liberation, Frederick Douglass's text is an important point of comparison for Jacobs and other women's narratives,.

Smith states that standard plot of the male-authored narrative can be seen "not only as the journey from slavery to freedom but also the journey from slavehood to manhood."[45] I would add that the narratives associate freedom with the end of constraints on particular capacities of the black body, and unsurprisingly, as the texts collapse freedom and manhood, freedom is associated with ending constraints on the capacities of the black body most associated with masculinity and ending the threats to the male body.

Douglass most certainly tells the story of his liberation as his movement from "slavehood to manhood," and that movement concerns ending constraints on his ability to attain education, his capacities for productive labor, and his capacities for speech and action—that is, political voice—as well as freedom from white physical violence. Smith argues that Douglass's narrative charts his maturity and presents that movement to manhood—"how a slave becomes a man"—in two stages. First he learns to read, an accomplishment that he credits with creating his desire for freedom.[46] Through the medium of the written word he learns of the concept of "freedom" and of the abolitionist movement. When he is well on his way to becoming a man, however, the process is forestalled when he is sent to the violent "slave breaker" Covey.

Recall that throughout the text Douglass observes the considerable physical threats to the body within the slave system, securing the narrative's status as a thoroughly modern text. His time with Covey brings those threats into sharpest relief. Douglass writes:

> I had been at my new home but one week before Mr. Covey gave me a very severe whipping, cutting my back, causing the blood to run, and raising ridges on my flesh as large as my little finger. . . . He then went to a large gum-tree, and with his axe cut three large switches, and, after trimming them up neatly with his pocket-knife, he ordered me to take off my clothes. I made him no answer, but stood with my clothes on. He repeated his order. I still made him no answer, nor did I move to strip myself. Upon this he rushed at me with the fierceness of a tiger, tore off my clothes and lashed me till he had worn out his switches, cutting me so savagely as to leave the marks visible for a long time after. This whipping was the first of a number just like it, and for similar offences.[47]

He goes on to say, "I lived with Mr. Covey one year. During the first six months, of that year, scarce a week passed without his whipping me. I was seldom free from a sore back."

In the texts white physical violence constrains the black body, forcing the body to make use of its capacities for productive labor for white benefit. Douglass describes his time as a field hand for Covey thus:

> Long before day we were up, our horses fed, and by the first approach of day we were off to the field with our hoes and ploughing teams. . . . We were often in the field from the first approach of day till its last lingering ray had left us; and at saving-fodder

time, midnight often caught us in the field binding blades. . . . [Covey] would [nap in the afternoons] then come out fresh in the evening, ready to urge us on with his words, example, and frequently with the whip.[48]

White violence also functions to deny the body use of its capacities for speech, it silences the political voice of the enslaved. This violence, then, is the obstacle to manhood, and overcoming that violence ends constraints on the body's capacities for speech and productive labor.

Douglass's stalled journey to freedom does not begin again until he bests Covey in a physical contest well suited to the mythic status it subsequently attained. Douglass secures his manhood—his freedom—once and for all through reciprocal violence. Indeed, once Douglass bests Covey he is finally a man: "This battle with Mr. Covey was the turning point in my career as a slave. It rekindled the few expiring embers of freedom, and revived within me a sense of my own manhood."[49] Smith writes, "If the acquisition of literacy first enabled him to feel free, the act of physical resistance precipitates his second and lasting period of liberation."[50] It is worth noting that this physical violence not only serves to secure the body, it heals that body, it even heals the soul, redeems it, so that it is no longer fallen. Douglass not only becomes a man, he is resurrected: "It was a glorious resurrection, from the tomb of slavery, to the heaven of freedom."

Feminists have noted that Douglass famously glosses over sexual violence against women in the text. Tate says that "[o]nce Douglass had sympathetically ascribed the female 'other' as the object of sexual abuse, he abandoned that topic in favor of abstract humanist abolitionist arguments that drew heavily on the republican discourses of the American revolution."[51] Put another way, once he mentions the threats to the female body and aspects of the black body most associated with femininity, he moves on to focus on the body's capacities for speech and action. He presents no liberation, no redemption for the female body or for the capacities of the black body most associated with femininity and the material labors that have come to define the feminine in the text.

Male-authored narratives reference, but do not contain a sustained focus on, the gender-specific threats to the female body, the slave system's constraints on the aspects of the body and the material labors most closely associated with femininity. Female-authored narratives make these constraints central. Harriet Jacobs's narrative is an important case in point.

Jacobs was born into slavery in Edmonton, North Carolina in 1813. She fled the institution in 1835, moving to New York City in 1842, where she began working for the abolitionist cause. Washington, Smith, Carby, and Tate have all analyzed the ways in which Jacobs transformed the slave narrative—complete with its republican ideals and conceptions of domination and freedom—so that it might best accommodate her story of bondage and liberation. Tate holds that Jacobs "privatizes" the slave narrative, stating that in order to do this she made a key structural change to the genre, importing plot devices from the sentimental fiction popular in the period in which she wrote, and thereby opening up a space to discuss the threats to the female body and the constraints that the system placed on the powers and capacities of that body. Her decision was not without critics: John Blassingame dismisses the narrative entirely, not only for its inability to represent the slave experience, but doubting its very authenticity—because of the narrative's extensive treatment of her constraint within the sphere of intimate relations.[52]

Jacobs merges the two genres in an effort to shift the focus from the struggle to liberate the black body from physical assault that functioned to compel that body to use its productive labor capacities for white benefit and to silence its capacities for speech, to focus instead on sexual assault, as well as severely constrained and coerced reproduction under conditions of maternal dispossession. The purpose of this merger is to tell a story of liberation apart from a quest for manhood.

Jacobs's narrative of bondage is a tale of sexual harassment, sexual assault, and frustrated maternity; free life would begin for her the moment she escaped her master's sexual demands and arrived at a place where "no hand but that of death" held power over her children.[53]

Jacobs's comparisons between a free life and a life in bondage concern the capacities of the body most closely associated with femininity and the material labors that have come to define the feminine. A free woman, for example, exercises unconstrained choice and has the power to consent to sexual relations. Jacobs speaks of and to "happy women," "who have been free to choose the objects of your affection," as she relates her own tale of woe:

> If slavery had been abolished, I, also could have married the man of my choice; I could have had a home shielded by the laws; and I should have been spared the painful task of confessing what I am now able to relate; but all my prospects had been blighted by slavery.[54]

Free women also have unconstrained caretaking capacities and hence unconstrained relationships with their children. Speaking again of and to "happy free women" Jacobs states:

> O, you happy free women, contrast your New Year's Day with that of the poor bond-woman! With you it is a pleasant season; and the light of the day is blessed. Friendly wishes meet you everywhere, and gifts are showered upon you. Even hearts that have been estranged from you soften at this season, and lips that have been silent echo back, "I wish you a happy New Year." Children bring their little offerings, and raise their rosy lips for a caress. *They are your own and no hand but that of death can take them from you.* [emphasis mine]. But to the slave mother New Year's Day comes laden with peculiar sorrows. She sits on her cold cabin floor, watching her children who may be torn from her the next morning; and often does she wish that she and they might die before the day dawns. She may be an ignorant creature; degraded by the system that has brutalized her from childhood; but she

has a mother's instincts, and is capable of feeling a mother's agonies.[55]

Jacobs presents the central tragedy of slavery as the frustrated maternity that is the plight of the female slave. She relates the tale of the slave mother whose children have all been stolen from her:

> One of these sale days, I saw a mother lead seven children to the auction-block. She knew that *some* of them would be taken from her; but they took *all*. The children were sold to a slave trader, and their mother was bought by a man in her own town. Before night her children were far away. She begged the trader to tell her where he intended to take them; this he refused to do. How could he, when he knew that he would sell them, one by one, wherever he could command the highest price? I met that mother in the street, and her wild, haggard face lives today in my mind. She wrung her hands in anguish, and exclaimed, "Gone! All gone! Why *don't* God kill me?" I had no words where with to comfort her. Instances of this kind are of daily, yea, of hourly occurrence.[56]

This scene is repeated in other slave narratives, but represents a particularly important moment within female narratives.[57]

Jacobs does not rest content with her lot. She makes her master's sexual harassment and sexual abuse the focal point of her resistance. This struggle began far too early in her life, as her master, Flint, began "people[ing her mind] with unclean images" early on in her teenage years. She was resolved, however:

> I was determined that the master, who I so hated and loathed, who had blighted the prospects of my youth and made my life a desert, should not, after my long struggle with him, succeed at last in trampling his victim under his feet. I would do anything, everything for the sake of defeating him.[58]

She first attempts to exercise choice regarding sexual partners by asking to marry a free black man, a request her master denies. She then temporarily prevails against her master's advances by taking another sexual partner—a white man—and she explicitly connects this admittedly severely constrained choice in sexual partners to freedom in a heartbreaking statement, saying "There is something akin to freedom in having a lover who has no control over you, except that which he gains by kindness and attachment."[59]

Jacobs' own severely constrained choice regarding her sexual relationships was also engineered to afford her greater power over any children she might bear, as her master sold the products of his sexual relationships with enslaved women, and often the women themselves.

> I shuddered to think of being the mother of children that should be owned by my old tyrant. I knew that as soon as a new fancy took him, his victims were sold far off to get rid of them; especially if they had children. I had seen several women sold, with his babies at the breast. He never allowed his offspring by slaves to remain long in sight of himself and his wife. Of a man who was not my master I could ask to have my children well supported; and in this case, I felt confident I should obtain the boon. I also felt quite sure that they would be made free.[60]

The relationship, then, was also a part of her efforts to ensure, as far as she could, that "no hand but death" could take her children. Jacobs's statements regarding how important her children were to her was not idle talk. She demonstrated that her children were a central part of her understanding of her own freedom: scholars have often marveled at the fact that she postponed her own escape for seven long years until she could secure freedom for her children:

> I could have made my escape alone; but it was more for my help-less children than for myself that I longed for freedom. Though

the boon would have been precious to me, above all price, I would not have taken it at the expense of leaving them in slavery. Every trial I endured, every sacrifice I made for their sakes, drew them closer to my heart and gave me fresh courage to beat back the dark waves that rolled and rolled over me in a seemingly endless night of storms.[61]

I should note that Jacobs's actions here are in line with historical evidence regarding female resistance patterns in the period of enslavement. Women demonstrated considerable concern for the welfare of their children, a fact in evidence in Gray White's survey of ads searching for female runaways. Of 151 fugitive women advertised for in New Orleans newspapers in 1850, she says, "none was listed as having run away without her children."[62] Their concern for child welfare seems to have impacted their resistance efforts in other ways as well, as women often favored short absences over running away altogether. "Truancy seems to have been the way many slave women reconciled their desire to flee and their need to stay."[63] She goes on to say that "Studies of female runaways demonstrate that females made the most likely truants because they were more concerned about breaking family ties."

Jacobs ends her story as follows: "Reader, my story ends with freedom; not in the usual way, with marriage. I and my children are now free!"[64]

Thus while Douglass's narrative foregrounds a struggle for liberation from physical violence and focuses on the constraints the system places on the black body's capacities for productive labor and political speech and action—that is, threats to the male body and constraints on the capacities of the black body most closely associated with masculinity—liberation from sexual and reproductive violence that paves the way for unconstrained choice in sexual partners and unconstrained relationships with children are emphasized in Jacobs's narrative—the specific threats to those who possess feminine embodiment, the capacities of the body and the material labors that have come to define the feminine.

Returning to the infanticide, we can now better consider the event and its backdrop in light of the themes highlighted in the narratives above. The historical record reveals that Garner married her husband at fifteen. The couple did not cohabitate and saw each other only on weekends. After the birth of their first child Garner began to give birth to biracial children, and evidence suggests that her owner, Archibald Gaines, fathered the children.[65] Garner herself was described as "mulatto," and her father was most likely another member of the Gaines clan.[66] In the event's backdrop, then, we observe sexual violation—that is, constraints on Garner's ability to make choices regarding sexual partners—and coerced reproduction—her inability to choose whether or not she reproduced and with whom. In truth we see a female subject whose sexual, reproductive, and caretaking capacities are subject to direct use and control within the slave system. We see this female subject strain at this use and control, and then there is the deed.

It is unsurprising that Garner's story has attained mythic status for black feminist scholars. Here within the events surrounding an attempted escape—that form of resistance to enslavement most associated with men, as they were far and away the largest population of runaways, and a course of action often associated with resistance to the particular forms of use of the black male body within the institution—the resistance project for female intimate capacities, arising out of the women's distinct embodied experience, resulting from the slave system's particular investment and use of the black female body and the unique desperation of the slave mother is completely visible and invites interpretation. Those constraints most significant to Jacobs eclipse those that most exercised Douglass. The resistance in the intimate sphere that enslaved women undertook—that is, the struggle to perform sexual, reproductive, and caretaking activities without constraint—and the place of this struggle within the black liberation and subsequent black freedom project as a whole take center stage within the dramatic events unfolding in the story. The events leading up to the infanticide direct attention to two types of bonds. One is the foreclosure of civic bonds between black and white men inaugurated by the total control and use of the black body by the whites, those bonds being replaced by violent, even deadly relations. The other concerns the less remarked, but concurrent, use and control of the capacities of the black female body most closely associated with femininity—its capacities for engaging in sexual relations, reproduction, and care. The system's demand for total control of the female body wrought havoc on the bonds of the embodied female subject with her intimate partners and children, and those bonds were replaced by furtive, volatile relations, complete with a desperate fugitivity. Here we see the black intimate sphere-at-large. And then, in the most dramatic turn of events—a turn powerful enough to take precedence over the lost civic bonds that generally receive the lion's share of interest and interpretation in male-authored texts—the violence "coded as female" responds most decisively—most violently—to the constraints on the black body.

In the course of events surrounding the infanticide we also observe what Spillers identifies as the "dual fatherhood" set in motion, "the African father's *banished* name and body, and the captor father's mocking presence."[67] We see Robert's absence in biological reproduction. The captor father is not physically present in the climactic scene—no skin in the game, as it were—but he is certainly there, spectral. And although Robert is physically present, and he is certainly subject to physical violence, he is without violated sexual, reproductive, and caretaking flesh; his body has not been subject to the particular forms of use that take center stage here.

Even as the extended family makes the escape, and in the climactic scene where Robert is aiding his family, his embodied experience of enslavement can be distinguished from that of his wife. We have no evidence, as we do with Margaret, that sexual and reproductive oppression was a significant aspect of his enslavement; we have no evidence, as we do with Margaret, that his master raped him. We have no evidence that he was forced to procreate, and we know that he was not forced to provide care under conditions of dispossession, under severely constrained, violent, volatile conditions, as Margaret was. Significantly, he did not attempt to end the lives of his female children, but shot back in the form of violent self-defense that is well recognized and enshrined as an appropriate form of resistance against identifiable agents of racial domination and racialized constraint. Therefore, while I acknowledge that the story is very much a story of partner collaboration, it is partner collaboration that is most focused on the forms of use to which the slave system subjected the female body most centrally, and this is why it so speaks to black women.

In this most dramatic scene within the early black freedom struggle, only Margaret's body is "there." Or, as Spillers so elegantly states, "In this play of paradox only the woman stands *in the flesh,* both mother and mother dispossessed."[68] Margaret has the embodied experience of sexual assault, dispossessed reproduction, and constrained and insufficient caretaking. She lives in the body forced to reproduce—forced to use the reproductive capacities of her body to carry, sustain, and produce a being- -but powerless to determine what it is that she produces.

Let me pause to say that I do not want to give the impression that the conditions I highlight did not affect and injure Robert and others like him. I do, however, want to counter emphatically and absolutely the tendency that Darlene Clark Hine has noted to interpret female sexual abuse and sexual and reproductive violence, constraint, and exploitation, through the eyes of men alone, and how the men must have felt to witness sexual assault and exploitation, as if women are only the tools in efforts to emasculate men and not subjects who were themselves hurt.[69] I instead want to focus on the embodied experience of those who were there *in the flesh* and the potential for an embodied liberation for black female sexual, reproductive, and caretaking flesh that we see in women's responses to sexual violation, dispossessed and demeaned reproduction, and caretaking.

TOWARD A BLACK FEMINIST THEORY OF FREEDOM

"In this play of paradox only the woman stands *in the flesh*, both mother and mother dispossessed." Tragic, but lest we think all is lost, Spillers also sees empowerment potential created in this "mother and mother dispossessed"—in fact, she says that the creation of the "mother" and "mother dispossessed" opened up a potential point of insurgency that feminists should seek to retain. Again, I think Hirschmann is useful in thinking about how we might actualize the empowerment potential today in order to retain the insurgent ground, as not only does her feminist conception of freedom help us clarify what we are to make of the infanticide, it is also an important part of what is necessary for bringing about freedom for black women today. The slave system, in trying at once to dispossess the mother and deny the child—the latter with the institution of the *partus sequitur ventrem*, wherein the condition of the mother was "forever entailed on all her remotest posterity" and thus her children would always in some important sense be hers—unwittingly created a "different female social subject," a mother with the "potential power to name."[70]

In her discussion of William Goodell's understanding of the *partus sequitur ventrem* Spillers notes that Goodell, like Frederick Douglass and like Daniel Patrick Moynihan so many years later, sees a mother with the power to name as the principal degradation of slavery. Spillers, of course, sees it otherwise:

> But what is the "condition" of the mother? Is it the "condition" of enslavement the writer means, or does he mean the "mark" and the "knowledge" of the *mother* upon the child that here translates into the culturally forbidden and impure? In an elision of terms, "mother" and "enslavement" are indistinct categories of the illegitimate inasmuch as each of these synonymous elements defines, in effect, a cultural situation that is *father-lacking*. Goodell, who does not only report this maxim of law as an aspect of his

own factuality, but also regards it, as does Douglass, as a fundamental degradation, supposes descent and identity through the
female line as comparable to a brute animality.[71]

She goes on to say:

> This problematizing of gender places [the mother and mother
> dispossessed], in my view, *out* of the traditional symbolics of
> female gender, and it is our task to make a place for this different
> social subject. In doing so, we are less interested in joining the
> ranks of gendered femaleness than gaining the *insurgent* ground
> as female social subject. Actually *claiming* the monstrosity (of a
> female with the potential to "name"), which her culture imposes
> in blindness, Sapphire might rewrite after all a radically different
> text for a female empowerment.[72]

A mother—a woman—with the potential power to name. This is
no small thing, particularly given that Hirschmann points out that
within patriarchal cultural contexts women are not only unable to
make some choices and compelled to make others, unable to choose
X so they make do with Y, unable to choose whether to engage in
sexual intercourse or not, whether to give birth and rear children or
not—but they are also constrained by the fact that men have had all
power in determining the meaning of their actions, the meaning of
X and Y, naming X and Y.[73] Women have had less power to determine
the meaning of what they do. Men have made the laws, customs, and
rules of appropriate behavior that are simply imposed on women and
restrict their choices.

Enslavement, in addition to being an exploitative system of
social control and coerced labor that systematically constrained black
women's ability to make choices regarding their intimate lives, also
constrained black women's meaning-making power regarding those
intimate lives. Thus, in addition to constraining her power to make
decisions about her sexual partners and sexual intercourse itself, her
power to reproduce and provide care, a significant aspect of Garner's

enslavement concerned her "de-meaned" sexuality, reproduction, and caretaking.

Garner, forced to reproduce for her master, lost control of the sexual, reproductive, and caretaking capacities of her body *and* her ability to name the meaning of her actions associated with those capacities. Most interpreters understand that in her act of resistance she meant to claim that the products of those capacities would be hers to name the meaning thereof or they would not be. They certainly would no longer be named by slaveholders who had until then held far too much power in both the biological creation *and* the meaning creation of her children. She resolves this conflict—tragically, pyrrhicly, to be sure—with the infanticide. Ultimately, while problematic, the infanticide remains so powerful because of Garner's decision as a dramatic and desperate move to have final say over the meaning of her sexual, reproductive, and caretaking actions.

Additionally, beyond the problem of meaning creation, Hirschmann's feminist account of freedom also helps us to see another aspect of the infanticide with important implications for thinking about what freedom could have possibly meant for enslaved women and as well as what it might mean for black women today. We can see the infanticide as highlighting the necessity of striking out against the internal, against that which is "somehow internal."[74] Why, however, would that be necessary?

Hirschmann argues that mainstream freedom theorists tend to be overly concerned with identifiable agents of constraint—here with the slave master, and later, for black women, sterilizing doctors and other agents of population control—agents who would stand in a person's way, in a woman's way, and not allow her to act as she willed. They have typically conceived free action as a formula where person A is free to do X because person or institution B does not prevent him from doing X. On this formulation enslaved women were not free because slave masters directly intervened and did not allow them to choose whether or not to have sex, whether or not to reproduce, whether or not to provide care. As Isaiah Berlin famously stated, "I am normally said to be free to the degree to which no man or body of men interferes with my activity."[75] On this view, where there is no slave master (no doctor who forcibly sterilizes, no judge who orders long-acting contraceptives), black women are free to exercise the sexual, reproductive, and caretaking capacities of their bodies that had been so constrained in the period of enslavement.

These theorists have given considerably less attention, Hirschmann says, to cultural and contextual barriers that shape women's desires and function just as effectively to limit women's freedom of action. Mainstream liberty theorists have no problem identifying how a sexual harasser, an abusive partner, a rapist, a slave master, or a sterilizing doctor impinges on women's freedom, but she holds that a social context in which sexual harassers, abusive partners, rapists, slave masters, and sterilizing doctors act with impunity, where they go unpunished, creates a climate of fear that can function just as effectively to limit women's freedom of action. If women do not go out at night because they are dissuaded from doing so by fear of being raped, for example, they are constrained because of a general power that limits their freedom of action, and no less so because the power that restrains them is not exercised by a particular man.

A part of the problem that leaves negative liberty theorists insufficiently attuned to the problem of the internal is that they have labored to secure liberty for a discrete, naturalized subject who arrives at the point where he makes his decision—and arguably into the world itself—with full knowledge of all the choices he could make, uninfluenced by his surroundings, not unlike Douglass and Jacobs. She holds that, instead, an adequate conception of freedom must be attentive to issues that have concerned only positive liberty theorists historically and that absolutely terrified Berlin. Those include internalized constraints that are significant because they are actually manifestations of social and institutional contexts. For Hirschmann, any choice to do X is in reality "a complex process of negotiation and relations between what we commonly call 'internal' and 'external' factors, between will, desire and preferences and forces that not only inhibit or enable the realization of such desires but also contribute to or influence the formation of this desire."[76] Garner's love for her

61

child, her all-too-human desire to see the child safe, as we know, had been created wholly against her will in a racist and sexist social context. Tragically, to be free she could not strike out only at the external forces—at the posse at the door as Robert did—but she would have to confront that which was internal.

Because context has such an important impact on the formation of desires, Hirschmann holds that "women's exercise of agency and freedom thus requires the help of others, the positive liberty focus on the potential of others to help one realize one's true self and desires." Hirschmann maintains, then, that women require both greater negative and, contra Berlin, greater positive liberty and an understanding of freedom itself that is attentive to the contexts in which women act that negative liberty theorists in particular ignore, in order to be free. Hirschmann holds that "if context sets the terms for understanding claims of freedom and if women's choices and opportunities, desires and options exist within a context of patriarchy, we have good reason to believe that sexism itself can act as a barrier to freedom."[77]

Hirschmann illustrates her point through an examination of the social context in which women experience domestic violence. She says that, while we might see a woman "choosing" to go back to an abusive partner as making a choice, she sees it as a woman enacting a social expression of the value we give to women in this situation. Police, for example, are likely to emphasize the difficulty of prosecution, how a partner is unlikely to be punished and may further harm the victim in retaliation for her efforts to seek help. Police are also only one link in a chain of authority figures in a woman's life, including family and clergy, who act to dissuade her from moving forward in cases of domestic violence and who influence the choices that she makes in a way that is inconsistent with affording her freedom of action. Our institutions do not support her leaving, so what choice does she really have?

> Because police fail to arrest, women stop calling the police, because courts do not convict, women become reluctant to press

charges or testify, because emergency personnel either fail to help adequately or report abuse to state agencies, women stop seeking medical attention, because friends and relatives tell them, along with the rest of society, that women are responsible for making relationships work and because battered women themselves share these beliefs and hold themselves responsible for the welfare of their batterers, battered women are ashamed of their abuse and do not tell anyone about it or ask for help.[78]

Hirschmann holds that we must, therefore, attend both to external barriers to women's freedom of action and to what she calls women's internalized constraints, which she says are the product of sexist social conditions and contexts on women's psyches, identities, and self-conceptions.

Hirschmann also uses the example of rape to illustrate her point. As previously noted, she says that if women do not go out at night because they are dissuaded from doing so by fear of being raped, they are constrained by a general power that limits their freedom of action, and no less so because it is not exercised by a particular man. Women who fail to act or who considerably revise their plans for action because they look out onto a (racist) sexist social context and do not see the help they need to realize their aims cannot be considered free. Freedom for women, then, requires transforming the (racist) sexist social contexts in which they act so that those context provide the help they need. Providing said help will remove any internal barriers to liberty.

I agree with Hirschmann, but I want to point out several things to think about going forward as we thinking about how all women can be afforded genuine freedom. First, women bear neither the burdens of sexist social context, nor the internal constraints created by those sexist social contexts equally. Take the issue of domestic or intimate partner violence. In *Arrested Justice* Beth Richie helps to paint a picture of how vastly different the contexts in which many black women live are from white social contexts and what this means for black female victims of intimate partner violence. Richie says:

> According to most national studies African American women are disproportionately represented in the aforementioned data on physical violence against intimate partner. In the violence against women survey, 25% of black women had experienced abuse from their intimate partners, including "physical violence, sexual violence, threats of violence, economic exploitation, confinement, isolation from social activities, stalking, property destruction, burglary, theft and homicide."[79]

Richie goes on to say:

> The research has not only established a higher incidence rate of intimate partner violence for black women when measured statistically, but also a greater impact of that violence.... Factors such as the limited availability of crisis intervention programs, the greater likelihood of a weapon being used against a black woman during an assault, and a lack of trust in law enforcement agencies may heighten some women's vulnerability to intimate partner violence.[80]

The problem is not only more acute for black women, but calling the police when they experience violence exposes them to potential criminalization and not simply neglect, as police violence is a part of a continuum of male violence under whose threat they live. The higher incidence, the greater severity of the violence, the greater likelihood of weapons as well as the potential for police violence all make supplying the help they need an intersectional issue, as helping white women and helping black women will not look the same.

On the issue of rape, black women, too, are unequally burdened in this regard. Richie states that many black women are living, working, schooling and worshipping in degrading, dangerous and hostile environments where the threat of rape, embarrassment and public humiliation are defining features of their social environments. The incidence of rape is higher in these communities and women are assaulted in more brutal ways. The women also live in communities wholly devoid of the help they need—they always have and still do—communities with fewer support services and fewer safe housing options should they experience violence.

Richie presents evidence of the divergent sexist social contexts in which black and white women live. The contexts in which black women reside have a far more urgent need for anti-sexist reform.

So one important aspect of women's unequal constraints across race is directly related to the problem of the racialization of space. Conditions in black space are far more marked by violence and the threat of violence, because of what Lisa Miller has called longstanding racialized state failure and what Richie sees as currently exacerbated by the rise of America's prison nation—something, I want to point out, that the Jacobs narrative does a very good job of highlighting.[81] My point here is that we must understand that the sexist social contexts in which women act are also racialized spaces, and we must recall that black and white women actually rarely occupy the same kind of space,. This was the case for Jacobs and Garner and it is the case for black women today. Sociologists Ruth Peterson and Lauren Joy Krivo, for example, have found that most black women live in neighborhoods with "levels of disadvantage," as sociologists refer to it, that white women, no matter how poor, never experience. The authors do not hide their own surprise that in the United States there can be no comparison between black and white social worlds, given how distinct white and black neighborhoods are. Thus a crucial point for any feminist theory of freedom is the recognition that white and black patriarchal cultural contexts are wholly distinct with regard to resources, security provision, police presence, community violence, and levels of disadvantage. Contemporary black social contexts are shot through with the violence, disinvestment, and racialized uneven development that has always attended life on the dark side of modernity, while white communities are far more secure. Transforming the sexist social contexts in which black women act into enabling spaces will require considerably more resources in light of this situation.

I would also note, specifically, that black women are wholly unlikely to look out into their social environments and see the help they need to exercise their sexual, reproductive, and caretaking capacities, such as they exist, and that this help is more likely to exist in white space. So, in addition to being constrained generally by domestic violence, community violence, sexual harassment, and public sexual aggression, they are also constrained by the peculiar features of American racial geography that also functions to limit their ability to exercise their intimate capacities. Enabling family support services are more likely to be present in white communities, while disabling and disruptive child welfare services that disproportionately remove black children from homes are features of black communities. (Dorothy Roberts refers to an "apartheid system of child welfare"). This pattern is also true with regard to enabling reproductive health services versus population-oriented contraceptive distribution in white versus black communities. Beyond this, because of America's racialized geography and racialized uneven development, white working mothers are able to work much closer to home than black working mothers, which enables white caretaking while functioning to disable such caretaking among blacks.

Furthermore, race and space are not responsible for all of the unequal burdens. If, as Hirschmann says, freedom theorists have not attended to how women might internalize the social value we assign to what happens to them, again rape is actually particularly distressing in terms of the social value we assign to violations of black female bodily integrity. In *Mapping the Margins: Intersectionality, Identity Politics and Violence against Women of Color*, Kimberlé Crenshaw cites a study of prison terms handed down to Dallas-area men convicted of raping women. The study found that the average prison term for raping a white woman was ten years, for raping a Latina woman five years, and for raping a black woman two years. [82] This speaks volumes regarding the relative value we assign to violations of women's bodily integrity across race. This must be changed, although restorative options in addition to punitive options should be explored here.

The second point I would make regarding Hirschmann's theory of freedom is that the necessity of a shift from impunity to punishment in the interest of black women's freedom is not as straight forward. Hirschmann suggests that freedom for women requires punishing those who violate women and who at present restrict their liberty with impunity. Affording women freedom requires ending impunity and holding those responsible for violations of women's liberty accountable. Of course, all who violate women should be punished nad punished equally, but who is ultimately responsible for the disproportionate violence to which black women have been subject historically and continue to experience today? Who is ultimately responsible for the higher incidence of rape, the greater brutality of those assaults and the lower likelihood of punishment for those violations? I hold that it is the American state and those so long empored to define the meaning of black womanhood, of a black woman as she who could not be raped, as she who was the proper target of violence and that state must be held accountable. The American legal system, serving the interests of its economic institutions, as well as white patriarchally constructed cultural norms have not been innocent regarding this social construction; stated plainly, the above are responsible. Black women, who only gained legal recognition of their bodily integrity after black feminist activism in support of this in the 1970s, after suffering decades of systematic sexual assault and sexual terrorism, continue to face harms that stem from the racist social construction of the meaning of black womanhood, of the black woman as someone who could not be raped.

Crenshaw says that rape-law reform measures that do not in some way engage and challenge the narratives that are read onto black women's bodies—the meaning of black women's bodies—are unlikely to affect the way cultural beliefs about black women oppress black women in rape trials, and she is absolutely right. Holding those who violate black women accountable would go a long way to reducing their internal barriers to liberty, but so too would the American state taking responsibility for its role in facilitating these violations of black female bodily integrity. I address this as an issue of corrective racial justice in chapter 5.

Saying sorry is not enough. Additionally—putting its money where its mouth is, so to speak—the state might provide resources for the deconstruction of the problematic meaning of black womanhood that facilitates the harms black women suffer, and the reconstruction of this meaning by black women. Freedom for black women from such severe violations of negative liberty as rape will require positive liberty–style support to deconstruct and then reconstruct the meaning of black womanhood. This might mean supporting black women's representational work—the work of black women and even black feminist filmmakers, storytellers, visual artists, and even advertisers. This will not complete the project of intimate justice—that, as I will argue below, will require the spatial rearrangement of black communities and transforming the geography of black urban space. It will require addressing transportation disparities for working mothers, providing enabling reproductive health care services, offering family support services, and providing security for bodily integrity. However, reconstruction of the meaning of black womanhood is also an important, and I think a necessary, step.

RACIAL VIOLENCE AND THE POST-EMANCIPATION STRUGGLE FOR INTIMATE EQUALITY

THE MOTHERS AND WIVES TRAINING SCHOOL RIOT OF 1890

In 1890, during the "nadir" of American race relations, a new school sparked a week of violence as a white mob terrorized the black community of Baton Rouge, Louisiana.[1] Racial violence was hardly noteworthy in this period. From 1882 to 1951, according to the most conservative estimates, 4,730 blacks were lynched in the United States.[2] Observers in the early part of the twentieth century witnessed the rise of the American race riot, a phenomenon of white-on-black violence that reached its apex in the "Red Summer" of 1919 when twenty such riots broke out in the United States.[3] Both the focused mob violence characteristic of lynching and the diffuse mayhem of the early-twentieth-century race riots have been characterized as systematic extralegal responses to black political and economic advances, a connection first made regarding lynching by Ida B Wells.[4] The Baton Rouge event commands our attention, however, because of the school's aims.

Baton Rouge's "White League," the group that claimed responsibility for the violence, demanded that missionary Joanna

Moore's "Mothers and Wives Training School" close. Evelyn Brooks Higginbotham writes:

> Despite the moralistic and prosaic image of mothers' training, some white southerners went to violent lengths to prevent black women from being taught the domestic ideals of whites. . . . Such was the case when the "White League" threatened Joanna Moore and the black female students at her school in Baton Rouge.[5]

In a note "embellished with a drawing of a skull and crossbones," the league made explicit the reason the school could not stand: "You are educating the nigger up to think that they are the equals of white folks."[6] The next day:

> [T]he League brutalized a black minister who lived nearby and supported Moore's work. The minister told [Moore] that a group of white men wearing "hideous masks" came to his house in the night. They beat him in front of his wife and children, who stood helplessly with pistols to their heads.[7]

This scene was not atypical. Many others were victimized, and members of the mob murdered one community member. The violence led many blacks to leave the city. Their flight created a labor shortage, which prompted "the good white people" of the community to intervene.[8] The riot was successful, however, as Moore closed her school and ended her work in Baton Rouge.[9]

Higginbotham does not fail to note that this is a puzzling case, complete with extreme violence in response to black women attempting to perform activities long considered mundane and stultifying, frankly often considered lower order concerns and even wholly insignificant in much of Western political thought. What was going on here?

Apart from what seems an extreme response to black women undertaking the most mundane of tasks, another reason the event is worth considering at length is that Moore's erstwhile students, forced to defer their domestic dreams, aspired to something that many of their immediate predecessors as well as their black female contemporaries also desired. Their enrollment was, for example, in keeping with a well-documented—what some scholars have referred to as a "near universal"—trend observed among freed women after Emancipation.[10] In a post-Emancipation context in which "[c]ontrol over one's labor and one's family represented a dual gauge by which true freedom could be measured," an overwhelming number of newly liberated women withdrew from the agricultural labor they had almost all performed within the plantation regime and devoted themselves instead to full-time care work for their families.[11] Yet although freed women demonstrated their desire to be, as Tera Hunter states, "mothers and wives first and laundresses and cotton pickers second," many whites disagreed.[12]

The riot demonstrates that some white supremacists made a direct connection between the sphere of intimate relations and racial equality. Higginbotham notes this, stating, "Moore's dictums on housekeeping, maternal and wifely duties, carried a message of black dignity and equality that did not rest well with white supremacists."[13] The riot is one example of militant resistance to black women devoting themselves to meeting the needs of the black body and to black women's explicit decisions to develop and exercise the capacities of their bodies most closely associated with femininity in an autonomous black intimate sphere. This is significant for us, for as we know, enslaved women were often compelled to exercise their bodies' capacities for brute force, with little time to meet the emotional and physical needs of partners and dependents—of developing and developed black bodies—nor to tend to their own physical and emotional needs and to have them met as well.

Nor was this violent white resistance to black women devoting themselves to meeting the physical and emotional needs of the black body an isolated incident. The reign of the notorious "I Am Committee" in middle Tennessee and Logan, Kentucky decades earlier is another case in point. In 1867, the committee put the aforementioned communities under martial law and used violence and intimidation to enforce their preferred racialized labor arrangements. They expressly denied blacks the ability to establish independent households and decreed that all black women must engage in labor for whites and never devote themselves exclusively to providing caring labor for their families, in explicit opposition to the withdrawal trend. As Hannah Rosen says, the group "insisted that black women subordinate themselves within and contribute their labor to white households only."[14] The *New York Times* ran a copy of the committee's demands, reprinted from *The Nashville Press & Times*:

A Copy of the infamous handbill, headed "I Am Committee," will be found below, taken from an original in our possession:

I Am Committee

1. No man shall squat negroes on his place unless they are under his employ, *male or female.*
2. *Negro women shall be employed by white persons.*
3. All children shall be hired out for something.
4. Negroes found in cabins to themselves shall suffer the penalty.
5. Negroes shall not be allowed to hire persons.
6. Idle men, women or children shall suffer the penalty. [Emphasis mine][15]

Again, the above were not mere aberrations in the period's vigilantism. Rosen's research revealed that "resistance to an independent domestic life among former slaves shaped the activities of later Reconstruction era gangs who would over time operate under the rubric of the KKK."[16] Thus night riders and other vigilantes—with tacit state support through inaction—terrorized the black intimate sphere in an effort to keep blacks, most pointedly black women, from devoting themselves exclusively to providing caring labor to black bodies. They threatened black women who would meet these needs and harassed them out of the sphere of intimate relations.

This demonstrates that whites employed violence to thwart blacks' efforts to enter all domains formerly reserved for whites. And while the dominant accounts of post-Emancipation racial violence foreground violence against men in civic space and, I would add, racial violence that aimed to deny blacks the opportunity to exercise the capacities of the black body most closely associated with masculinity, it is imperative that we hold in view an image of blacks terrorized and harassed—chased out of the realm in which the physical and emotional needs of the body are met - in much the same way as they were chased out of the public sphere in the period.

Beyond these violent incidents, the sentiments behind the Mothers and Wives School Training Riot and the I Am Committee's terrorism were widespread and the violence itself represented only one form—though a form that was at once widespread and rarely noted—of broader resistance to black women's attempt to withdraw from formal labor markets in order to care for their families. As we know from Hirschmann, violence was not the only means available to white supremacists for preventing black women from caring for their families. Specifically, black women also confronted a broader dissuasive culture in which the overwhelming message was that, if they were to tend to the needs of bodies, those bodies should be white. In addition to the militant resistance described above, the women also faced considerable white consternation and, often, outright ridicule. Eric Foner observes, "[m]any contemporaries who viewed white women at home as paragons of the domestic ideal saw their black counterparts as lazy and slightly ludicrous."[17] They took every opportunity, it seems, to mock and bemoan the freedwomen's efforts. For example, scholars who claim that freed women's attempted withdrawal from agricultural labor was a widespread phenomenon cite two sources, Freedmen's Bureau Reports and an 1869 pamphlet commissioned by cotton brokers Loring and Atkinson, *Cotton Culture and the South Considered with Reference to Emigration*.[18] The pamphlet is interesting reading. It provides several first-hand accounts from whites who observed the women's withdrawal, and the observers' reactions border on hysteria. Whites made no secret of their upset. In Danbury County, Georgia, for example, a man reported that "all the negro women are out of the fields, doing nothing." A respondent in Montgomery County, Texas, lamented, "The women have retired from the field, and prefer to make a precarious and vicious living than to work." In Baldwin County, Georgia, one interviewee, speaking of the poor black creatures and of how "the labor value of the free negro, as a cotton producer, is greatly impaired by his indiscriminate political privileges," also noted that "[a] remnant of labor yet lingers in the field, but daily diminishes: the women have quite retired, and so too have the children." A respondent in Oglethorpe County, Georgia predicted *"You will never see three millions bales of cotton* raised in the South again unless the labor system is improved. Why? Answer 1st. Because one-third of the hands are *women* who *now* do not work at all."[19]

Part of the complaints and ridicule regarding black women's withdrawal into familial caring labor concerned immediate, practical self-interests. Tera Hunter states, for example, that the historical estrangement of elite Southern white women from domestic labor was reflected in the very architecture of the South, as "the kitchen of many houses was a self-contained building in the backyard."[20] She goes on to say, "The stand-alone kitchen symbolized elite white women's alienation from the labor she had relegated to slaves."[21] Jacqueline Jones, a historian of black female labor force participation, reports that "[a]ccording to a South Carolina newspaper writer in 1871, the withdrawal necessitated a 'radical change in the management of [white] households as well as plantations' and proved a source of 'absolute torment' for former masters and mistresses."[22]

Finally, resistance to the withdrawal trend cannot be placed solely on the shoulders of white supremacists—both violent and non—as former abolitionists and white supremacists alike opposed black women's decisions to devote themselves exclusively to meeting the physical and emotional needs of the black body.

And white supremacists were not the only ones who took concrete steps—steps over and above lamenting the withdrawal in Southern newspapers—to reinstate and maintain the old order, wherein the needs of the black body remained neglected so that black women could devoet themselves to serving white bodies and white interests. Jones states:

> Many [agents of the U.S. Bureau of Refugees, Freedmen and Abandoned Lands] aimed to put into practice a view common among white Northerners, whether missionaries, Union military officials, Republican politicians, or transplanted migrants newly arrived in the South. These whites believed that, now that the Civil War had destroyed the institution of slavery, it was essential that black men and women return to the cotton, rice and sugar fields. . . According to this view, black women "worked" only when they labored under the watchful eye of a white person in a field, or in a kitchen, but not when they cared for their own families at home.[23]

That is, after the Civil War, in a period where there was little agreement between Yankees and Confederates, between abolitionists and white supremacists, they were in accord on the issue of "black women's place." Jones states, "one assumption they did share was that black wives and mothers should continue to engage in productive labor outside their homes."[24] The conflicts between Northerners and Southerners might center on whether or not the women would enter the lowest positions at a factory, remain in the rows of cotton dotting the landscape, or continue soothing white children, but one place they agreed the women did not belong was in their own homes caring for their families. The tasks most closely associated with the concept of black women's work were picking cotton and the most difficult, dirtiest, and least esteemed domestic labor in white homes, not tending to the physical and emotional needs of black households.[25]

White supremacists who held that black women should devote themselves wholly to meeting the physical and emotional needs of white bodies were also aided by a profoundly stratified labor market, which restricted black women's employment options to agricultural labor and caring for white bodies. White women, for their part, increasingly refused to perform what came to be understood as black women's work—the dirtiest and most labor-intensive domestic labor, including pre-mechanized laundry work, for example—and asserted exemptions from such labor both in their own homes and elsewhere as an important aspect of white privilege. And some working white women even engaged in collective action—in hate strikes where the demands were not for higher wages but that no black women be hired—in order to keep them out of emerging female-dominated but cleaner and less labor-intensive occupations such as department-store sales clerks—and capitalists largely complied. Their efforts were a resounding success. Economists Teresa Amott and Julie Matthaei note that from Emancipation to the 1960s black women were largely confined to domestic labor.[26] Therefore, even if it is true, as Heidi Hartmann says, that capitalism and patriarchy have enjoyed a long and healthy marriage in the U.S. context, capitalism definitely saw white women on the side.[27]

RACE RIOTS AND SEXUAL VIOLENCE: THE GENDERED AIMS OF POST-EMANCIPATION RACIAL TERROR

We must also understand this period as one in which whites violently resisted black female claims to bodily integrity, a fact which Rosen holds is often obscured in analysis of the period's racial violence. In addition to documenting and analyzing the I Am Committee's reign of terror, Rosen examines testimony provided in the aftermath of the Memphis Riot and Massacres of 1866, as well as the testimony of victims of racist vigilante groups provided to the Freedman's Bureau and other groups charged with assessing the extent of racial terror from 1866 to 1871.

The testimony reveals that freedwomen viewed their liberation from sexual servitude—their newly won right as emancipated beings to leave coercive sexual relationships with white men—as an important aspect of their freedom; for them, their new ability to refuse the commonplace sexual demands of white men represented a prized change in their status in comparison to their lives in slavery. Rosen says:

> Indeed, freedwomen seized the opportunity granted to them by federal forums not only to testify about postemancipation rape but also to document coerced sexual relationships with white men prior to the end of slavery. Their testimony reveals how new rights to refuse the demands of white men for sex, and thus to control their bodies and sexual relationships, were for African American women a central part of the meaning of freedom.[28]

For example, "[t]o Minerva, a forty-five-year-old former slave living in Murfreesboro, TN, being 'free' meant that she no longer had to accept lying 'in the same bed' with her former owner, D. Beasely, as she had done for seventeen years before the war."[29] Rosen goes on to demonstrate that this understanding of freedom was fiercely contested *and* that interpretations of racial conflict in the period tend to obscure this fact.

Violence against women wherein perpetrators expressly challenged black women's right to bodily integrity was widespread in this period, and yet it remains largely uninterpreted in favor of a focus on other forms of violence designed to stem the exercise of other black capacities. For example, black women were often raped during the period's race riots, but the "real" story is presented as a tale of masculine, civic racial conflict over black (men's) roles in the public sphere, as most accounts focus on the conflicts within interracial civil society, conflicts over emerging black male civic social roles. This is certainly the case regarding the most common readings of the Memphis Riot, Rosen says. In order to fill out the picture of all that was at stake in the riot, Rosen draws attention to several incidents during the riot that demonstrate that it must also be understood as a violent response to black women's claims to bodily integrity in addition to their new roles within an autonomous black intimate sphere closely associated with that integrity.

In order to appreciate the significance of riots to those who enact them, historians have examined patterns within the phenomenon and have concluded that, for riot participants, "certain ritual patterns fit their violence within a coherent symbolic context and endowed their actions with legitimacy and meaning."[30] Rosen observes that among scholars who interpret the "logic" of riots, the Memphis Riot has been understood in a variety of ways—as the reaction of white police and firemen to black soldiers stationed at Fort Pickering in Memphis, as a response to blacks' new status as agents of public authority, as a manifestation of labor competition, and as part of Irish efforts to become white through anti-black violence. But Rosen argues that the riot concerned more than this, and that most interpreters remain completely silent about the feminine half of the gender-specific violence within the riot. She states that "in these various efforts to interpret the political expression contained in the ritual patterns of this violence, the particular contours of sexual assault suffered by African American women remain largely unexplored."[31] For example, forty-eight blacks were killed and somewhere between seventy and eighty blacks were wounded in the Memphis riot of 1866. Rioters set fire to ninety-one freed people's homes and four black churches. This was not all:

They also burned down Caldwell Hall and threatened to burn the offices of the Freedmen's Bureau and of the *Memphis Daily Post.* They robbed at least 100 freedpeople and destroyed the food, clothing, furnishings, and other belongings of many more. And the assailants in the attack also raped at least 5 freedwomen.[32]

Specifically, members of the Memphis mob raped Frances Thompson and Lucy Smith after the women informed a group of five men who broke into their home and treated it like a brothel—demanding both food and sexual services—that they "were not that kind of women," that is, they were no longer enslaved women who were obligated to provide sexual and domestic services to white men on demand.[33] Other mob members explicitly denied Rebecca Ann Bloom's status as a wife when they broke into her home. The social role of wife and the home she shared were both important symbols of her life as a free woman; the attackers violated her home and expressly denied her right to choice in sexual relationships.[34] They took her husband from their marital bed. One assailant asked if she slept with white men and raped her when she proclaimed that she did not.

Rosen is also able to discern disturbing patterns in the period's sexual violence from freedwomen's testimony. Vigilantes would first solicit their victim's consent in an effort to maintain an important conceit of white supremacist ideology—that black women were incapable of refusing sex. When women refused consent and asserted the new female subjects they were—women who were no longer required to submit to the sexual demands of white men—the assailants then used force.

Rosen holds that the dialogue surrounding Bloom's assault, recorded in Congressional testimony on the riot, clearly reveals that it was an instance of retaliatory sexual violence in direct response to Bloom's claims to bodily integrity and her new status as a married woman living independently of whites, a woman who no longer existed solely to tend to the sexual, physical, and emotional needs of white male bodies. Bloom testified to the following:

On the night of the 2d of May 1866, I was in bed, when five white men broke open the door and came into my room and ordered a light. We had no candle. They took my husband out to get a light. One man remained in the room. He demanded my money. I had none. He wanted to know if I had anything to do with white men. I said no. He held a knife in his hand, and said he would kill me if I did not let him do as he wanted to do. I refused. He said, "By God, you must," and then he got into bed with me and

violated my person, by having connexion with me, he still holding the knife.[35]

The riot was not an isolated incident; sadly, the scenes from the
riot above were repeated throughout the period. It was a single
event in a broader climate of pervasive racialized sexual terror
where, as Hunter states, "organized sexual-assault raids against
black women" were common. Danielle McGuire writes, "The rape of
black women by white men continued, often unpunished, throughout the Jim Crow era. As Reconstruction collapsed and Jim Crow
arose, white men abducted and assaulted black women with alarm-
ing regularity."[36] These organized sexual assault raids were especially commonplace "in rural areas where the KKK thrived," but
urban blacks were in no way immune.[37] Elsa Barkley Brown reports
that in the wake of Emancipation, "[t]hroughout the summer and
fall of 1865 black Richmonders reported numerous violations of
their rights."[38] Brown examined testimony in Virginia Freedmen's
Bureau records and states, "Many [witnesses] spoke of the sexual
abuse of black women, of the 'gobbling up of the most likely looking negro women,' the women 'thrown into the cells, robbed and
ravished at the will of the guard.'"[39] She goes on to say that "[m]
en and women in the vicinity of jail testified to hearing women
scream frightfully almost every night."[40] McGuire writes that racialized sexual violence continued well into the 20th century as,
"During the 1940s, reports of sexual violence directed at black
women flooded into local and national NAACP chapters."[41]

THE JIM CROW BODY POLITICS/
JIM CROW BODY POLITICS: GENDER
AND THE STATE AS VIOLENCE
ENHANCEMENT MECHANISM

While violent direct intervention is not the only way whites blocked
blacks' access to spheres reserved for whites and blacks' exercise

of their capacities, it is a particularly important way, and one that looms largest in black political thought and the wider black political imagination. For example, Young holds that many contemporary theories of justice—focused as they are on resources—fail to consider and address the disproportionate violence to which members of oppressed groups are subject. The phenomenon of violence msut be addressed, she says, because the violence that members of oppressed groups face is systemic, not the aberrant behavior of a few rogue members of the political community, and is therefore a justice concern.[42] However, there has been no such lack of attention to the problem of violence within Afro-Modern thought.[43] It has long been and remains one of the most consistent topics of debate within the black public sphere and a concern that blacks repeatedly attempt to raise within the wider society. Scholars of anti-black violence have noted the shift from mob and vigilante violence to more institutionalized forms, including blacks' disproportionate experience of police brutality, but they are clear that the phenomenon remains.[44]

Analysis of the role of violence in the maintenance of racial hierarchy is one of Afro-Modern thought's most important contributions to modern thought more broadly. The relative significance of interracial violence as opposed to black marginalization within the productive economy, for example, emerged as a major source of contention among blacks—liberal, radical, and conservative—and mainstream American leftists in the early part of the twentieth century. Mainstream members of the left held that anti-black violence was a narrow racial concern and insisted on its confinement to marginal members of the white working class. Blacks contested this view, perhaps none so thoroughly as Du Bois. Many black members of the Socialist Party of America left the organization in 1919, for example, not coincidentally at a high point of racial violence. Black members of the SPA, the Workers' Party, and the Communist Party (CPUSA) all attempted to expand the mainstream left's thinking regarding race, questions of national liberation for oppressed groups, labor-union racism, and important nonindustrial categories of workers like black Southern agricultural laborers. Their disagreements also concerned the supposed backwardness of black workers, and therefore their need for white working-class enlightenment and stewardship, and whether or not the revolution would depend on the workers of Europe or those of Africa and Asia. But blacks, including Hubert Harrison, Cyril Briggs, W.A. Domingo, and perhaps none as effectively as W.E.B. Du Bois, consistently pushed the white left on racial violence, particularly on lynching and its effect on black economic life and black subjects' subsequent alienation. Here, Du Bois's contributions are one important case in point.

Cedrick Robinson, in his groundbreaking study of the history of the black radical tradition, holds that Du Bois was one of only two Americans—Sidney Hook being the other—who made significant contributions to Marxist thought in the twentieth century. Du Bois held that Marx provided an accurate analysis of labor relations in nineteenth-century Europe but thought that the analysis had to be revised in order to capture the specific conditions of labor in nineteenth-century America. In particular, he felt it necessary to analyze the role of peasants in revolutionary movements, the impact of racial ideology on class struggle and cross-class alliances—as white labor supported the institutionalization of the color line created by the elite planter class as well as white capitalists' imperial expansion efforts—and finally the role of mob violence within black/white labor and property relations, as the white working class made evident their steadfast support for the color line and even worked to sustain that line itself in labor relations and civic life more broadly through violence when given the opportunity. Therefore Du Bois, Robinsons says, expanded on the Marxist conception of oppression by attending to the significance of the phenomenon of mob violence within interracial labor relations.

Du Bois held that:

> Throughout the history of the Negro in America, white labor has been the black man's enemy, his oppressor, his red murderer, used to kill, harass and starve black men. White labor disfranchised Negro labor in the South, is keeping them out of jobs and decent living quarters in the North and is curtailing their education and civil and social privileges throughout the nation.

Du Bois observed blacks attacked on shop floors, run out of working-class neighborhoods, and chased out of public space. He went on to say that the Negro was

> sympathetic to efforts of workingmen to establish democratic control of industry and land, absolutely certain that as a laborer his interests are the interests of all labor, *but nevertheless, fighting doggedly on the old battle ground led by the NAACP to make the Negro laborer a laborer on equal social footing with the white laborer, to maintain the Negro's right to a political vote*, notwithstanding the fact that this vote means increasingly less to all voters; to vindicate in the courts the Negro's civil rights and American citizenship, even though he knows how the courts are prostituted to the power of wealth; and above all, determine by plain talk and agitation to show the intolerable injustice with which America and the world treats the colored peoples and to continue to insist that in this injustice, *the white workers of Europe and America are just as culpable as the white owners of capital*; and that these workers can gain black men as allies only insofar as they frankly, fairly and completely abolish the Color Line.[45]

Du Bois refuted the Socialists, and later the Communist Party's assertions, that white labor was driven to violence by ignorance, arguing that they had not demonstrated ignorance at all but rather calculating rationality. As well, their higher-ups moved immediately to institutionalize the color line in labor relations that the white mob demonstrated support for and helped to maintain, the two white classes working in tandem, happily extending the early efforts of the slaveholding planter class. Du Bois was particularly struck by the "hate strike" and other events wherein members of the white working class attacked blacks and not capitalists.[46]

Afro-Modern thinkers have devoted considerable attention to the impact of the phenomenon of racial violence and its role in the maintenance of racial hierarchy. However, the narrowly civic, and frankly masculine, focus that Rosen observes in most interpretations of the causes and "logic" of the Memphis Riot and Massacre is not atypical, as feminists have noted that far too often accounts of Jim Crow–era violence tend to marginalize violence against women. That is, despite the laudable attention that mainstream Afro-Modern thinkers have given to the role of violence in creating and sustaining racial inequality, feminists have remarked both their insufficient attention to the gendered dimensions of blacks' disproportionate experience of violence and the fact that the violence most closely associated with the male body and the masculine body's historic and present capacities has eclipsed violence that targets the female body most pointedly in symbolic significance. On the latter point Carby says, "the institutionalization of rape (as a technique of racial domination) has never become as powerful a symbol of black oppression as the spectacle of lynching."[47] This dominance is sustained even to the very end of Jim Crow. McGuire writes that although women wrote into NAACP offices and the Justice department regarding pervasive sexual assault:

> And yet analyses of rape and sexualized violence play little or no role in most histories of the Civil Rights Movement, which present it as a struggle between black and white men—the heroic leadership of Martin Luther King confronting intransigent white supremacists like "Bull" Connor . . . The histories of black women who fought for bodily integrity and personal dignity hold profound truths about sexualized violence that marked racial politics and African American lives during the modern civil rights movement. If we understand the role rape and sexual violence played in African American's daily lives and within the larger freedom struggle, we have to reinterpret, if not rewrite, the history of the civil rights movement.[48]

Lynching is recognized as a pillar—an institution of American racial democracy in a way that rape and sexual violence are not. The symbolic dominance of lynching is no small thing as it powerfully influences how we perceive the low point of American race relations and the high point of American racial violence as well as how we understand blacks' contemporary disproportionate risk of and exposure to violence. On the continuing symbolic significance of lynching, consider the following. After the deaths of Alton Sterling and Philando Castile, the artist Dread Scott hung a banner from the roof of the Jack Shainman gallery in New York that stated "A Man was Lynched by Police Yesterday," in direct reference to the banner that far too often hung from the window of the NAACP's New York headquarters from 1920 to 1938. If, when we think of blacks' longstanding disproportionate risk of and exposure to violence, we think of the violence most closely associated with the male body we are unlikely to take seriously ongoing significant threats to the black female body and the necessity of intersectional solutions to the problem of contemporary racial violence.

I recounted the scenes above in detail partly so that they will not be lost to history, so that we recall and reckon with this violence as well as its aims, that is, to diminish the black body's capacities to perform the "labor of the body" and to deny its capacities for bodily integrity. It is imperative that violence against women and the activities associated with femininity not be lost in discussions regarding the struggle for racial equality in the Jim Crow era, nor in discussions regarding corrective racial justice today.

I would argue that part of the reason for the symbolic dominance of lynching can be attributed to the strong association between lynching and white efforts to frustrate blacks' ability to exercise two prized capacities of the black body, its capacities for controlling its political and its material environment, two capacities greatly cherished by Du Bois and Washington, respectively - the two thinkers who, in the opinion of Cornel West, set the terms of national and even global discussion of black inclusion in the twentieth century[49] - and the strategic camps they represented, The dominance of lynching is linked to and reinforced by the prominence of these capacities of the black body in black political organizing and debate at the high tide of racial violence and to the association of sexual violence with what turn out to be lower-order capacities and concerns.

Adolph Reed summarizes the conflict between the two towering figures of Afro-Modern thought in the Jim Crow era as follows: "The central fault line separating [Washington and Du Bois] and the political tendencies they represented was the demand for black civic equality and political participation."[50] Gaines summarizes the strategic divide between Du Bois and Washington thus: "So-called 'radicals' (like Du Bois) advocated protest and agitation against lynching and disenfranchisement, demanding full citizenship rights; conservative leaders counseled accommodation, self-help, and the pursuit of property ownership."[51] The conflict, however, might also be summed up as a disagreement over which capacities of the black body should be prioritized within black political organizing—its capacities for speech, most closely associated with rationality, and the capacity which Aristotle held allowed man to communicate moral concepts and thus to participate in political life or its capacities for transforming its material environment. I hold that we can gain insight into what each thinker felt was most valauble about black subjectivity, about the black subject and what the black body itself could do and become and therefore what were the proper aims of politics full stop, what the political communit should most seek to protect and enhance. For Washington, organizing around the black body's capacities for reason and speech and, therefore, for political action in a hostile climate put that body at considerable and indeed unnecessary risk. Beyond that, recall, as well, that he pointed out the absurdity of the sight of a boy reading a French grammar book amidst a disordered and untended material environment.[52] Du Bois famously retorted that blacks were more than mere hewers of wood and drawers of water; they were, most importantly, rational beings who must be allowed to exercise their ability to communicate moral concepts through speech in the relam of politics. It is perhaps unsurprising that the period's foremost champion of comprehensive liberal arts education and enfranchisement for blacks evinces a hierarchical understanding of the body's capacities and, I would argue, most closely associated black humanity with its rationality. The overall point is that, in a context in which the body politic came together to diminish and endanger multiple capacities of the black body, the dominant camps within the period's black political organizing prioritized some of these diminished and endangered capacities over others.

I want to point out as well that it is not simply that the thinkers held the body's rationality and capacities for controlling its material environment above other capacities, it is also that DuBois, for example, conceived the labor of the black body—that is, all efforts to tend to the physical and emotional needs of the body, all labor necessary for the creation and maintenance of life itself, the labors that have come to define "the feminine," with which rape and sexual violence are so closely associated—as either at best simply functional and therefore capacities that were suitably instrumentalized in service of efforts to secure the more prized capacities, or at worst potentially wholly destructive of those political efforts to secure the higher capacities. For example, Cathy Cohen says of Du Bois's *The Philadelphia Negro* that in it the thinker falls within "a tradition of pathologizing the (sexual and reproductive) behaviors of the African American poor and working class, especially women"; she states that the same is true of more recent works, such as St. Clair Drake and Horace R. Clayton's *Black Metropolis* as well as "recent black community studies like those authored by Elijah Anderson and William Julius Wilson."[53] Cohen goes on to say:

> In defense of these authors and other similar texts, the fundamental objective of such studies, I believe, is to describe the contours of Black communities and to mount a rigorous examination of the systematic discrimination experienced by these subjects. However, far too often, as the researcher works to differentiate the lived conditions of segments of Black communities, internalized normative judgments about the proper and natural structure of family, intimate relationships and forms of social interaction creep into the analysis and prescriptions about what must be done. It is here, under the guise of objectively studying Black communities that the assumed importance of the nuclear family, appropriate gender relations, and the efficacy of the capitalist system imposes an understanding of difference that results in the pathologizing of all those who would choose differently on such fundamental and often assumed truths.[54]

For the Du Bois of *The Philadelphia Negro*, Cohen states that "[i]t was the absence of a strong nuclear family and its corresponding bourgeois sexual mores that aided systemic discrimination in destroying black communities."[55] What Cohen's analysis makes apparent is that Du Bois perceives not only a black body whose capacities are hierarchically organized but a black body potentially divided against itself, where the activities it undertakes and the capacities it exercises in the realm of sexuality and reproduction can only either support or derail what are presumably blacks' higher aims. This suggests that these capacities, in particular, are suitable for being instrumentalized—sacrificed as needed, elicited and even enhanced as needed—in service of the race's higher aims. Further, if they are not properly instrumentalized they are capable of working in tandem with white supremacy—the ultimate betrayal—to imperil the race. It is worth noting that Du Bois, unlike Aristotle,[56] does not instrumentalize women, does not see women themselves as functional; he considers only the capacities of the black body most closely associated with femininity as instrumental. This is enough, however, to create problems for all who would undertake the labors that have come to define the feminine—and, I would argue, those who possess feminine embodiment, as they reside in the threatening body, the body most closely associated with the capacities capable of derailing racial advancement. As we see from Cohen, he is not alone in this.

The symbolic dominance of lynching, then, reflects the hierarchical and indeed gendered ordering of the black body's capacities within the period's respective inclusionary projects, within the struggle for racial equality as Du Bois and Washington conceived it. Lynching's dominance reflects the greater significance Du Bois and the "radicals" attributed to the body's capacities for speech and political action so prized by Aristotle (and, as feminists note, held in opposition to "the feminine" by the ancient thinker[57]), as well as the greater significance Washington and the conservatives attributed to the body's capacities for transforming nature and the material environment so prized by thinkers like Locke and Marx (and also often set in opposition to the labors that have defined the feminine). The emphasis on lynching also reflects the very modern concern (arguably, that which puts the "modern" in Afro-Modern thought) for the general security of the black body from the threats inherent in living among other men—the threats posed in encounters with other men in civic space, associated with Hobbes, these threats greatly enhanced under racial domination. Sexual violence, as it is a form of violence associated with the least of the black body's capacities, simply cannot compete with lynching.

In what follows I would like to suggest that, in addition to Du Bois's hierarchical understanding of the body and its capacities, there are other things that should give up pause regarding how the thinker would "embody" racial equality as well as how those who undertake the labor that has come to define the feminine would fare under his vision of racial equality. First, the thinker was an advocate of women's political participation, but he also closely associates citizenship with manhood, with masculinity, and holds that the struggle for racial equality requires blacks to suppress "the feminine" in racial equality efforts, wherever it be found. Must black women become men, then, raising only masculine concerns, in order to participate in public life? And, will all aspects of their bodies be protected and secured equally in the interracial body politic to come? On this point we should be troubled by the work he understands sexual assault and the threat of sexual assault to do in creating an "efficient" black womanhood, presumably the ideal female citizen. Finally, can women truly be equal citizens if they reside in the body most associated with the very capacities that are capable of working in tandem with white supremacy to destroy all that blacks work for?

DUBOIS: CITIZENSHIP AS MANHOOD, RIDDING THE BLACK BODY POLITIC OF THE FEMININE, AND THE BURDENS AND BENEFITS OF SEXUAL VIOLENCE

Feminists do not agree about Du Bois and his legacy. Joy James, for example, gives the thinker a mixed review. She notes the disconnect between his impressive early advocacy of women's rights and his problem with female leaders in general—Wells and Cooper in particular. He failed to give Wells due recognition for her anti-lynching activism and marginalized her within the NAACP. James also notes the problematic "nonspecificity" in his nonfiction writings about women, which stands in stark contrast to the detail he provides regarding male elites; one infamous example that continues to upset feminists is his decision to cite Cooper without attribution in "The Damnation of Women."

Farah Jasmine Griffin is more laudatory. She acknowledges that black feminist assessment of Du Bois's legacy has not been monolithic, stating that pioneering black feminist scholars, including Beverly Guy-Sheftall and Claudia Tate, have struggled to come to terms with his personal sexism alongside his lofty ideals regarding women. For all his faults, however, Griffin believes that Du Bois deserves credit as an early bright light in women's-rights advocacy. She states that "more than any other African American thinker of his time or before, Du Bois devoted a great deal of his attention to the conditions of black women specifically and distinct from black men." She states that his arguments on behalf of black women "are most apparent in four works: the poem 'The Burden of Black Womanhood' (1907) and the essays 'The Black Mother' (1912), 'Hail Columbia' (1913) and 'The Damnation of Women.'"[58] Griffin thinks in particular that Carby's criticism, to which I turn below, may well have taken Du Bois aback, as he understood himself to be a "champion of black women and progressive on issues important to their advancement."[59] Lawrie Balfour agrees with Griffin's assessment of the thinker, stating: "That so many of the pieces in *Darkwater* exhibit a preoccupation with the past, present and future meanings of black women's experiences indicates the importance of those experiences to Du Bois's thinking at the height of his popular influence."[60]

Griffin lauds the fact that Du Bois championed an economically independent womanhood and a woman with the ability to control her fertility; the latter, she says, is an understanding of reproductive freedom that was even more progressive than that of many of his female contemporaries. Du Bois indeed argued that "[t]he future woman must have life, work and economic independence. She must have knowledge. She must have the right of motherhood at her own discretion."[61] Griffin goes on to argue that this celebration of female independence helped Du Bois see the limits of what she calls "the politics of protection" and its problematic contract between the male protector and female ward.[62] On the politics of protection Griffin states, "Because black women were denied the privileges of femininity and protection from physical and discursive violence, black intellectuals and activists developed a discourse of protection."[63] Du Bois did not fall into this trap, she says, as he argued the problems could be solved "[n]ot by guarding the weak in weakness, but by making weakness free and strong."[64] Ultimately Griffin's advice to black feminists is this: "Despite Du Bois's contradictions, we ought to learn from his limitations and mistakes and move on."[65]

Lawrie Balfour also praises the thinker. She argues that Du Bois makes an important contribution to a feminist theory of citizenship:

> "Damnation"'s contribution to a feminist theory of citizenship emerges from Du Bois's interweaving of three themes. First, he builds from the history of black women's sexual exploitation an expansive notion of sexual freedom that includes the freedom to have and to raise children regardless of marital circumstances. Second, he celebrates the economic independence achieved by African American women, making it a model, rather than a cautionary tale, for other women, and he does so without reinforcing bootstrap narratives of individual success. Third and finally, "Damnation" both advocates the inclusion of African American women as full citizens and acknowledges their historical importance as political actors, even in the absences of recognition by the polity.[66]

Griffin and Balfour make excellent points. For example, I concede that *Darkwater* differs from the racial-mahood obsession of a text like *Souls*. And the Du Bois of *Darkwater* deserves credit for his attention to and progressive views regarding the status and structure of the realm where the physical and emotional needs of the black body are met. It is not simply progressive, it represents genuine progress from the thinking of the Du Bois of *The Philadelphia Negro*. However, I see no evidence that he changes the relative esteem in which he holds the black body's capacities.

On Balfour's claim regarding Du Bois's support for women's full citizenship and the acknowledgement he gives to women as political actors, I would argue that the ambivalence James identifies between the thinker's advocacy of women's rights and his unease with women in civic space shows up in the text in ways that must be acknowledged as well. It is not simply that he noted what black women had achieved, in political protest work and arts and letters, for example, but how he assessed his black female coworkers in the kingdom of culture, particularly the accomplishments of the "strong, primitive types of Negro womanhood." He speaks of Phyllis Wheatley's "slight" muse, a muse only capable of inspiring "trite" verse. He speaks of the "to some degree mentally unbalanced" Tubman—"a woman with smiling countenance, her upper front teeth gone"—and he speaks of the "unsmiling Sybil" Sojourner Truth. I would argue that this list—when compared to his list of great black men—evinces little faith in women's ability to make contributions within what were for him the all-important realms of protest politics and arts and letters.

But even if we give Du Bois the benefit of the doubt and take him at his word regarding how he felt about women's suitability for political participation, how should we reconcile this with the strong connection he drew between the struggle for citizenship itself and manhood in *Souls*—where real men refused to submit and fought for citizenship, where manliness was necessary for gaining entry into the public sphere—and his hostility to feminine submissiveness in the racial-equality struggle personified in the figure of Washington? Must women behave like men to participate in the struggle for racial equality and, finally, as citizens?

Carby says of *Souls* that it was a project designed to write blacks into the American nation but that it was, at base, a masculine place he sought. It is a place, as well, that blacks can only secure if they remain vigilant and openly hostile to the feminine. And why should they not, as to behave as women do is to betray the racial-equality project itself? Recall that in "Of Mr. Booker T. Washington and Others," Du Bois presents a completely masculine set of protesters fighting against tremendous odds for inclusion into the American body politic. He criticizes Washington's program of political concession in exchange for economic advancement as unmanly, indeed, as womanish, and woefully out of step with a proud history of black masculine agency and assertive male protest against racial domination. He presents a list of great black men and juxtaposes the masculine assertiveness of Toussaint Louverture, Nat Turner, the maroons, and other rebels with Washington's submissiveness—most evident in his willingness to compromise, to submit, to white authority. Du Bois also argues that before Emancipation the struggle against racial domination took place solely on two fronts. There was, first, a group of men in the South who worked to liberate themselves from coerced productive labor so that they might freely transform their material environments, and then a second group of Northern men who fought to exercise the black body's capacities for speech and action. After Emancipation he states that all blacks came to understand that racial equality meant political participation and would labor to win these "manhood rights," either as integrationists in the tradition of Douglass, William Wells-Brown, and William Cooper Nell or in the nationalist tradition of Alexander Crummell and Martin Delany until the aberrant Washington's arrival on the national stage.

Must women, then, become men, complete with only male desires, fears, and concerns in order to enter the struggle for citizenship? In order to be citizens? Consider his statements in "Damnation"—and quite in line with the earlier Du Bois - regarding the kind of female citizen the race requires:

> Not being expected to be merely ornamental, they have girded themselves for work, instead of adorning their bodies only for play. Their sturdier minds have concluded that if a woman be clean, healthy, educated, she is as pleasing as God wills and far more useful

than most of her sisters. . . . Consequently, for black women alone as a group, "handsome is that handsome does" and they are asked to be no more beautiful than God made them, but they are asked to be efficient, to be strong, fertile, muscled and able to work.[67]

This certainly establishes that the right kind of woman for race work is she who does not worry about "girlie" things.

I also want to point out that while Du Bois is unequivocal that mob violence against blacks is bad, he presents a more equivocal account of sexual violence. Specifically, there is cause for alarm regarding the role of sexual assault and the threat of sexual assault in creating the right kind of black woman, the black woman described above, the appropriate black female subject for the racial-equality struggle:

> The result of this history of insult and degradation has been both fearful and glorious. It has birthed the haunting prostitute, the brawler and the beast of burden, but it has also given the world an efficient womanhood, whose strength lies in its freedom and whose chastity was won in the teeth of temptation and not in the prison and swaddling clothes.[68]

Shockingly, the sexual violation that black women experience, and that poses a constant threat, here becomes not women's damnation but a crucible of sorts that, when the temperature and black feminine material are just right, produces a more efficient womanhood. Thus, although Du Bois begins "Damnation" lamenting the sexual assault of black women as something he would never forgive, he also seems to think this violence has served a positive function historically, as it helps to create the efficient and useful (non-girlie?) womanhood the race needs to fulfill its aims. This raises questions regarding how well the female citizen's body will be protected: perhaps without this ever-present threat, even if the dream of racial equality is realized, the dreaded feminine creep back into the efficient black female subject.

The above should certainly give us pause, but perhaps most troubling of all - even if they are able to suppress the feminine - can women ever be trusted? After all, the female citizens reside in a body so closely associated with capacities that can only either support or threaten the race and its higher aims that one wonders if they can ever be equal citizens.

THE BLACK FEMALE BODY AND THE JIM CROW BODY POLITIC

In light of the above I want, first, to echo the point many feminists have made here and state that Jim Crow—the iconic period in which whites employed extralegal violence in an effort to maintain racial inequality—is most often presented in a way that marginalizes violence against women. It is presented as a racialized regime that aimed most pointedly at distorting civic relations among men, in order to thwart the development and exercise of the black body's capacities for speech and action and its ability to transform its material environment. For example, Du Bois's student Rayford Logan coined the term "the nadir." In his article, "The Historiography of the Struggle for Black Equality since 1945," Kevin Gaines states:

> The historian Rayford Logan certainly had disfranchisement in mind in the 1950s when, following the crushing defeat of wartime struggles for equality, he referred to the Post-Reconstruction period as the nadir, or lowest point, of African American history. Logan's term encapsulated the brutal system of racial domination that followed Reconstruction's demise. That system was characterized by disfranchisement, legal segregation, and the widespread practice of lynching—the mob execution of African Americans in the absence of the rule of law.[69]

Gaines himself offers the following definition of Jim Crow:

> Commonly known as Jim Crow, this system enforced by law and custom the absolute separation of blacks and whites in the

workplace, schools, and virtually all phases of public life in the South. ... Jim Crow segregation confined the majority of African Americans to a state of economic peonage as agricultural workers, making wage-earning jobs of the New South industrial order a whites-only economic preserve. Between 1890 and 1906, blacks were eliminated from the political arena as southern states amended their constitutions to deny blacks the voting rights that had been guaranteed by the Fifteenth Amendment (1870). Disfranchisement was enacted and enforced with the widespread use of violence, including lynching, to terrorize blacks from exercising political activism. As legally-sanctioned forms of racial exclusion, Jim Crow segregation and disfranchisement defined southern (and national) politics well into the twentieth century, until the Supreme Court's *Brown v. Topeka Board of Education* (1954) decision declared "separate but equal" unconstitutional, and the Voting Rights Act (1965) outlawed restrictions on the suffrage.[70]

In his description of the context in which Du Bois wrote *The Souls of Black Folk*, Gooding-Williams defines Jim Crow as a "homegrown form of racial apartheid that developed in the United States between 1890 and 1910" and as:

[a] relentless assault on black people's dignity that helped to stiffen a form of economic subjugation by which white landowners and industrialists controlled southern black laborers—the vast majority of whom were sharecroppers, bound to the land as tenants by a cycle of debt, giving half their crop to a landowner or furnishing merchant and eking out a difficult living with the other half.[71]

He goes on to say that blacks "who challenged this system of political and economic oppression quite frequently met with the terroristic violence of lynch mobs that injured and killed with impunity."[72]

Their characterizations are not incorrect, they are simply incomplete. The violence in the nadir of American race relations indeed included countless skirmishes over black participation within the formal political and economic spheres, over blacks' ability to exercise their capacities for speech and political action and their capacities for controlling their material environment. Formal political participation and access to the prevailing political routines were extremely important in black life after slavery. According to Eric Foner, "in 1867, politics emerged as the principal focus of black aspirations."[73] This was so much the case that Foner writes, "By the end of 1867, it seemed, virtually every black voter in the South had enrolled in the Union League or some equivalent local political organization."[74] Blacks also focused their energies on economic opportunity and property acquisition. Political organizations like the Union League often supported freedmen's economic interests, "not least by making members, as many whites complained, 'impudent' and assertive in dealing with their employers." Foner quotes one laborer as telling the future Alabama governor George S. Houston, "I have all the rights that you and any other man has, and I shall not suffer them abridged," after the laborer was evicted for attending a league meeting.[75]

And, as we are aware, whites reacted to black efforts in these arenas with violence, including politically and economically motivated assassinations and property confiscation. Lynchings formed one part of a cultural context in which, as Joy James states, "[r]acialized anti-black atrocities became routine rituals as whites sought to remove African-Americans from economic and political power." The ritual extralegal violence functioned alongside the inequitable dual legal code to force blacks into political and economic subservience and dependency.[76] While generalized white-on-black brutality accounted for some violence in the post-Reconstruction era, historian Nell Irvin Painter states that "[r]adicalism and political independence, however, accounted for a disproportionate part of the slaughter." She goes on to say that this "[e]xtralegal violence served primarily to keep Blacks in line politically," and that "the practice persisted throughout the rest of the nineteenth century, as long as Black voters—or maverick white ones—sought to exercise their suffrage in their own interests."[77] And so remaining inoffensive in the eyes of whites became necessary for survival, and not giving offense meant renouncing political organization and voting. "Politics increasingly became white folks' business" in a political context wherein, as Painter quotes one man as saying, night riders "disastered dem what meddled wid de white folks."[78]

Black participation in the free market also put them at risk of violence, as "the punishment in several states for blacks attempting to sell crops on the open market was whipping or assassination." This form of punishment became typical throughout the lower South in the period Painter examines.[79] In the period, then, "lynchings were part of a terrorist campaign in an undeclared racial war to destroy the newly won independence of the free black community."[80]

For all of its importance, however, the violence mobilized in the interest of thwarting the black body's capacities for speech and action and exercising control over its material environment has come to dominate the narrative of white resistance to black advancement in the Jim Crow period. Sexual violence, if it is mentioned at all, is most certainly presented as a lesser concern, as something adjunct. And should sexual violence register, this direct and targeted violence against the female body and its associated capacities can often be wholly subsumed under the banner of violence against the black male subject, as it is often interpreted as indirect violence against the masculine subject and its capacities and significant only in that it harms him. As Kimberlé Crenshaw puts it, "To the limited extent that sexual victimization of black women is symbolically represented within our collective memory, it is as tragic characters whose vulnerability illustrates the racist emasculation of black men."[81] The black female body, the embodied black female subject, is only at risk, only in any danger at all, because of her proximity to the masculine subject, indeed to the masculine project, to the exercise of the capacities of the black body most closely associated with masculinity.

Yet beyond simply echoing Carby, Crenshaw, Rosen and McGuire's critiques of dominant accounts and interpretations of Jim Crow–era violence, I want to suggest that we consider these critiques alongside feminist crtiques of the modern state and its theoretical architects. The latter thinkers can help us consider what it ultimately means to marginalize this violence, the imact of such marginalization and help us to think about how we should go about addressing the history of this long marginalized violence in the present. Moira Gatens holds that "[t]he political body was conceived historically as the organization of many bodies in to one body which would itself enhance and intensify the powers and capacities of specifically male bodies."[82] We should think of the Jim Crow body politic, by contrast, as having done the opposite, or more accurately it was Janus-faced for blacks and whites.[83] I argue that it is useful to think of the Jim Crow body politic and even the American state in this era and beyond as the opposite of Hobbes's conception of the modern state, as a violence enhancement mechanism for blacks. And here, accounts of Jim Crow violence that marginalize violence against women should be read as problematically and misleadingly presenting a Jim Crow body politic which sought only to expose male bodies to risk and to diminish the capacities historically associated with masculinity in blacks.

In light of the problematic conceptual construction of the modern body politic, Gatens invites us to consider the following:

> Suppose our body politic were one which was created for the enhancement and intensification of women's historical and present capacities. The primary aims of such a body politic might be to foster conditions for the healthy reproduction of its members.[84]

I would interject that, with regard to the American body politic as a whole and the Jim Crow body politic in particular, a collection of bodies not only came together to protect and enhance the bodies of white men, it allowed, facilitated, participated in, and even enhanced unchecked harms to the bodies of black men (and women), specifically denying them the protection from physical violence that the modern state was designed in part to provide, a protection it did provide to whites. This violence, which first took the form of mob violence, transitioned over time to police brutality, federally sponsored redlining, and other policies that confined black bodies to underprotected and insecure neighborhoods. For blacks, the state never functioned as the kind of violence-prevention mechanism envisioned by Hobbes—it has done the opposite, in fact—while it has done a great job of preventing such physical violence for even poor whites. While this may not have been its primary aim, in the Jim Crow era in particular the body politic functioned as a collection of bodies that came together—that could come together at any moment—to enhance the violence perpetrated against the black body, to expose the black body to risk, and to diminish the capacities of black bodies.

I would go on to point out that Gatens's dream of a state that affords protection and enhancement to women's historic and present capacities has actually been partly true for white women and it has certainly been the case relative to black women in the United States. This state, again, has served as a violence-enhancement mechanism for black women which functioned to diminish the capacities historically associated with them. The Jim Crow body politic came together to enhance the sexual violence enacted on black female bodies. The American state, for its part, facilitated violations of black female bodily integrity by creating and upholding a legal definition of rape that excluded black women, which in turn helped to create and reinforce the meaning of a black female body as a body that could not be raped. It propounded violations of black female bodily integrity by allowing the alignment of sexual violence and the profit motive in slavery, so that slaveholders had an economic incentive to violate black female bodily integrity. After Emancipation it did not intervene to correct a racially rigged market that confined black women to work in white homes, which exposed them to sexual violence from white employers. It allowed violations of bodily integrity to continue by failing to intervene to stop such violations even when black women were ostensibly covered by laws against them. It also propounded those violations by concentrating blacks in under-resourced and insecure communities.

The American body politic and economy have also actively helped to redistribute the benefits of the caring labor of blacks to white bodies, thereby facilitating the healthy reproduction of white members of the body politic, enhancing white women's historical and present capacities at the expense of the healthy reproduction of its black members, and they have done so in a context in which they have provided far greater security to white bodies overall relative to blacks. If the American body politic has not done all that it can for white women—a point I concede—it has certainly provided far more protection and enhancement to the intimate capacities of white bodies associated with femininity and allowed those of black women to be diminished and exposed. Problematically, however, when the state as violence-enhancement mechanism is presented as most pointedly diminishing and exposing the male body, it allows the enhanced harms to female bodies to remain unchecked and unaddressed.

As stated above, Robert Gooding-Williams uses the term "Afro-Modern" to denote a genre of modern political thought. For Gooding-Williams a key point of distinction between Afro-Modern political thought and its modern counterparts, including the social-contract tradition, is that works within the former are less concerned with the legitimate and properly restrained power of the state and more concerned with outlining the political and social organization of successive regimes of racial domination. But although Gooding-Williams draws attention to significant differences, there are also important similarities. A concern for the safety and security of the body, for example—a concern the "somatophobic" Plato would have found "womanish"—is one such important similarity, for example, between Afro-Modern thought and the work of Thomas Hobbes.[85]

This point of similarity is understandable, as anti-black violence exposed the black body to heightened risks in interactions with others. It is thus unsurprising that the tradition shares important features with Hobbes, who was haunted by the insecurities of state breakdown and civil war.[86]

But there is another troubling point of similarity, namely the similarities in the state-of-nature story and traditional accounts of Jim Crow–era racial domination. Feminists have noted that state-of-nature stories arose in the minds of European men, who sought a place for themselves in forming a government in order to secure property and person, to free themselves from paternalistic and absolutist authority. The stories revealed what the thinkers cherished and feared most and what they would wish to protect and enhance in constructing a state. Feminist political theorists have noted that male embodiment figures prominently here. Gatens, for example, says, "the modern body politic is based on an image of a *masculine* body which reflects fantasies about the value and capacities of that body."[87] I would add "what is valued about that body." She goes on to say, "the relationship between the public sphere and male bodies is not an arbitrary one. The political body was conceived historically as the organization of many bodies in to one body which would itself enhance and intensify the powers and capacities of specifically male bodies."[88]

Gatens notes that Hobbes, for example, privileged the concerns of the male body over those of the female one and sought to create a powerful state to protect and enhance the bodies of men. Hobbes himself says as much when he proclaims, "For by art is created that great LEVIATHAN . . . which is but an artificial man, though of greater stature and strength than the natural for whose protection and defense it was intended and in which the sovereignty is an artificial soul, giving life and motion to the whole body."[89] Gatens continues, "Man in a state of nature, he tells us, is in 'continual fear' and in 'danger of violent death' and the quality of his life is summed up with the words 'solitary, poor, nasty, brutish, and short.'"[90] Gatens goes on to say that for Hobbes the state is a work of "creative artifice" analogous to the creation of man by God that explicitly uses the male body image. It is presented as a product of reason, motivated by fear designed to administer, manage, and govern the needs and desires that arise out of the bodies of the male subject.

Gatens argues as well that the modern body politic is not only symbolically male, but legally so; by using male bodies as the model for the lives its legal and political arrangements are designed to protect, it marginalizes the desires and needs of the female body and the concerns of women. Modern states give little attention to—have only "the occasional surrounding legislative insets concerning"—such issues as abortion, rape, and maternal allowances.[91] As such, female embodiment continues to present an obstacle to citizenship when the model citizen is male. "Female embodiment as it is currently lived," she says, "is itself a barrier to women's 'equal' participation in socio-political life."[92] Importantly, such gendered obstacles would not exist if the state were constructed on a different model of embodiment.

This privileging of the male body is crucial to keep in mind when thinking about our racial past and about corrective racial justice in the present, where our vision must never be modeled on the male body alone—marginalizing the capacities, desires, and needs of the female body—and where the forms of violence we seek resources to stem are not those most closely associated with the male body alone. This is why the similarities between the state-of-nature tale and the construction of the modern body politic, on the one hand, and traditional accounts of Jim Crow, on the other, both of which focus primarily on the uncertainties men face in their dealings with other men in civic space and in their efforts to control their material environments, should concern us, and why we should reject this view of the matter. The desires and fears that thinkers have foregrounded in traditional accounts—the forms of violence they consider most significant, the metonymy of the phenomenon of lynching, that part of violence against the black body thought sufficient to represent the whole—are important, as are the capacities of the black body which thinkers present as having been most threatened and diminished under racial domination. They are important because the story they tell forms the blueprint for how they would "embody" racial equality and racial justice, which capacities they consider essential in bringing about raical equalitn and racial justice; it determines the capacities of the black body for which they most pointedly seek recompense. And that should leave us with serious concerns as to how those who do not possess masculine embodiment will fare under these projects so embodied. There may be under these arrangements, resources permitting, minor insets of the kind Gatens observes in the modern state regarding rape, sexual violence, and other threats to the female body, and minor provisions, if any, for those who would undertake the labor that has come to be associated with the feminine, so that they might see their lot somewhat improved, but these bodies, these capacities, would most certainly not be given priority over other presumably more important bodies, more significant capacities. And, as I suggest with Du Bois above, these capacities—those capacities of the body most closely associated with femininity and the material labors that have come to define the feminine—would remain in danger of being instrumentalized in the service of the race's higher aims regarding its ostensibly higher capacities.

Feminist political theorists have noted that social-contract theorists labored most pointedly to free man in civic space but had no desire to free women, no desire to make sweeping changes to the sphere of intimate relations; they freed themselves from paternalistic authority in civic life, leaving paternalistic relations among men and women in domestic space largely unchallenged.[93] Correspondingly, in traditional Afro-Modern thought's insufficient attention to and acknowledgement of the violence that targeted the female body specifically and the state's role in facilitating that violence, they would leave that form of anarchistic and indeed enhanced violence against the black body and its associated capacities unchallenged and unaddressed while the male body is freed. Gatens writes: "In the absence of a female leviathan, natural woman is left unprotected, undefended, and so is easy prey for the monstrous leviathan. Like the hapless Jonah, she dwells in the belly of the artificial man, swallowed whole, made part of the corporation not by pact, not by covenant, but by incorporation."[94] The black feminine subject as well could be incorporated into the interracial body politic, as unprotected in interracial civil society as she was in the racialized state of nature that was Jim Crow.

I would like to close the chapter by considering the nonhierarchical ordering of the capacities of the black body offered by thinkers like Anna Julia Cooper and her fellow clubwomen, as well as an account of a group of women who might be defined as their rivals, blues women thought about the intimate capacities of the black body.

Du Bois's female contemporaries, for their part, did not evince this hierarchical understanding of the black body's capacities and therefore, while not all were perfect, suggested a different model for how we might "embody" racial equality and corrective racial justice. Their approach inspires me as I consider how we might embody corrective racial justice, and so I turn to them below.

'. . . FOR THE SAKE OF ALL HUMANITY, WHICH IS MORE THAN ANY ONE SECTION OF IT": THE STRUGGLE FOR A PERFECTLY RESPECTABLE AND A COMPLETELY OUTRAGEOUS BLACK INTIMATE SPHERE

Carby names the last decade of the nineteenth century as the first golden age of black women's writing and activism, pushing back against the tendency in Afro-Modern thought to consider the period the age of Du Bois and Washington alone. She says, "Though Afro-American cultural analysis and criticism have traditionally characterized the turn of the century as the age of Washington and Du Bois, the period was in fact one of intense activity and productivity for Afro-American women."[95] Stated another way, the protection and enhancement of the black body's capacities for speech and action and the work of its hands and the hierarchical view of the black body that undergirded these organizing aims alone did not exhaust black political organizing in the period. Anna Julia Cooper explicitly challenged the tendency among the period's male leadership to speak of racial progress without reference to clear setbacks regarding black female bodily integrity, that is their tendency to privilege other capacities over black's bodily integrity in thinking about racial equality. Part of Cooper's legacy, then, is a vision of a black body whose capacities are not hierarchically organized but given equal consideration.

Elizabeth Alexander argues that Cooper's *A Voice from the South* is an innovation within the genre of the political essay. The books' essays insert black women's experiences, particularly Cooper's own, into the discourse of Afro-Modern political thought. She continued a tradition of innovation within the black political narrative inaugurated by Jacobs, Alexander says, "by writing her body into the text."[96] While Jacobs imported plot devices from sentimental fiction into the slave narrative genre to address the gendered aspects of her enslavement, Cooper retained the primary concerns of the female slave narrative—a focus on the impact of racial domination on the sphere of intimate relations—and inserted them into the discursive realm of late-nineteenth-century Afro-Modern political thought.[97]

Cooper is most famous for arguing against the ascendant "manhood" project in racial-uplift ideology, stating that the progress of the race could not be measured by the progress of its men alone, and "that only the black woman can say when and where I enter."[98] She spoke out against an understanding of racial progress conceived strictly in terms of the civic achievements of individual men—here measured only with reference to the exercise of the body's capacities for speech and action and transforming its material environment alone. There could be no progress, there had been no black progress, in a world that permitted the sexual violation of black women. We should understand her, then, as someone who refused an understanding of a black body divided against itself, a view that might allow women's advancements regarding the work of their hands to be divorced from the insults, violations, and degradation of the labors of their bodies.

Cooper paints a vivid picture of the threats to the female body within the violence-enhancement mechanism that was the Jim Crow body politic:

I would beg, however, with the Doctor's permission, to add my pleas for the *Colored Girls* of the South:—that large, bright, promising, fatally beautiful class that stand shivering like a delicate plantlet before the fury of tempestuous elements, so full of promise and possibilities, yet so sure of destruction; often without a father to whom they dare apply the loving term, often without a stronger brother to espouse their cause and defend their honor with his life's blood; in the midst of pitfalls and snares, waylaid by the lower classes of white men, with no shelter, no protection nearer than the great blue vault above, which half conceals and half reveals the one Care-Taker they know so little of. Oh, save them, help them, shield, train, develop, teach, inspire them![99]

Cooper goes on to argue for the necessity of devoting collective resources—positive liberty style resources—for protecting the bodies of black women:

I see not why there should not be an organized effort for the protection and elevation of our girls such as the White Cross League in England. English women are strengthened and protected by more than 12 centuries of Christian influences, freedom and civilization; English girls are not dispirited and crushed down by no such all-leveling prejudice as that supercilious caste spirit in America which cynically assumes "A Negro woman cannot be a lady." English womanhood is beset by no such snares and traps as betray the unprotected, untrained colored girl of the South, whose only crime and dire destruction often is her unconscious and marvelous beauty. Surely then if English indignation is aroused and English manhood thrilled under the leadership of a Bishop of the English church to build up bulwarks around their wronged sisters, Negro sentiment cannot remain callous and Negro efforts nerveless in view of the imminent peril of the mothers of the next generation. "I am my sister's keeper!" should be the hearts response of every man and woman of the race and this conviction should purify and exalt the narrow, selfish and petty personal aims of life into a noble and sacred purpose.[100]

It is important to see this not as Cooper engaging in the politics of patriarchal protection—as both women and men should be involved in these protection efforts—but correctly pointing out that said integrity is not natural and requires positive liberty style support and protection for its realization, particularly within the Jim Crow body politic, with its heightened sexual violence. Here she is effectively arguing for a black female leviathan, a force to protect the bodies of black women.

Cooper's was not an isolated voice. Indeed, from 1890 to 1895 many black women formed clubs throughout the country. They often did so after a visit from Wells during her anti-lynching campaign, but the clubs "owed their genesis to the peculiar circumstances of black life in general and specifically to discrimination against black women"— to the particular threats to which the black female body was subject.

By 1896 black women had created a national organization, a federation of clubs around the country "to confront the various modes of their oppression," the National Association of Colored Women (NACW).[101] Davis states:

> It was in response to the unchecked wave of lynchings and the indiscriminate sexual abuse of Black women that the first Black women's club was organized. . . . When the First National Conference of Colored Women convened in Boston in 1895, the Black clubwomen were not simply emulating their white counterparts, who had federated the club movement five years earlier. They had come together to decide upon a strategy of resistance to the current propagandistic assaults on Black women and the continued reign of lynch law.[102]

The proximate cause of the groups coming together was an editorial written in 1895 by James W. Jack, president of the Missouri Press Association, to Florence Belgarnie of England, Secretary of the Anti-Slavery Society. Jack stated that "the Negroes of this country were wholly devoid of morality, the women were prostitutes and were natural thieves and liars."[103] The piece mobilized "an army of organized black women," in the service of "self-sacrificing young" teachers and the "noble army of mothers who had given birth to them," in a sustained effort to defend the dignity of both, and undertaken "for the sake of our own dignity, the dignity of our race and the future good name of our children."[104] In her address at the First National Conference of Colored Women, Josephine St. Pierre Ruffin stated:

> Too long have we been silent under unjust and unholy charges; we cannot expect to have them removed until we disprove them through ourselves. It is not enough to try and disprove unjust charges through individual effort that never goes any further. . . . Now with an army of organized women standing for purity and mental worth, we in ourselves deny the charge and open the eyes of the world to a state of affairs to which they have been blind, often willfully so, and the very fact that the charges, audaciously and flip-pantly made, as they often are, are of so humiliating and delicate a nature, serves to protect the accuser by driving the helpless accused into mortified silence. It is to break this silence, not by noisy pro-testations of what we are not, but by a dignified showing of what we are and hope to become that we are impelled to take this step, to make of this gathering an object lesson to the world. . .Our wom-en's movement is woman's movement in that it is led and directed by women for the good of women and men, for the benefit of all humanity, which is more than any one branch or section of it.[105]

The NACW's considerable membership rolls provide clues as to the organizational aims and protest movements that commanded wom-en's allegiance in the period, and indeed to the significance of the capacities of their bodies most closely associated with femininity in their visions of racial equality. The NACW's membership rolls rival Marcus Garvey's United Negro Improvement Association. By 1918 the group's membership was 300,000 strong.

Of course, not all women organized against sexual violence. Some saw fit to leave the South instead, and Darlene Clark Hine states that black women's experiences of sexual violence were also significant non-economic factors in their migration decisions.[106] In fact, sexual violence often preceded economic opportunity among women's deci-sions to migrate—that is, the labor of the body took precedence over improvements regarding the work of the hands—as "[s]econd only to black women's fears of sexual violation is the pervasive theme of the frustration attendant to finding suitable employment."[107] Those who left the South altogether, then, migrated not only in search of economic opportunity but in search of bodily integrity as well. Yet again, Hine notes, that those motives are often overshadowed by a focus on men's migratory responses to male on male violence and men's frustrated agency regarding politics and employment.

But among those who organized, Hine says that "at the core of essentially every activity of the NACW's individual members was a concern with creating positive images of black women's sexuality."[108] Hine sees the establishment of the NACW as the institutionalization of the "culture of dissemblance," important among a variety of black women's responses to pervasive sexual terrorism.

Hine begins her text on the development of a post-Emancipation "culture of dissemblance" among black women by reflecting on Carby's claim that rape never became as powerful a symbol of black oppression as lynching.[109] She argues that "[r]ape and the threat of rape influenced the development of a culture of dissemblance among Southern black women," that is, the women developed "a politics of silence," "a cult of secrecy," to protect the sanctity of the inner aspects of their lives.[110] The broadly held belief that black women were incapable of refusing demands for sex and therefore incapable of being raped took its toll. In one effort to counter negative stereotypes regarding their sexuality, "many black women felt compelled to downplay, even deny, sexual expression."[111] The women, then, sought to downplay their sexuality in order to protect it.

The NACW's efforts to end pervasive sexual violence against black women and racial terrorism designed to thwart the formation of an autonomous black intimate sphere have been rightly criticized for "policing, sanitizing and hiding the nonconformist behavior of blacks,"[112] and for seeking to protect black female sexuality and bodily integrity by restraining black female sexuality and the black female body itself. Members more often than not espoused Victorian gender roles and norms regarding appropriate behavior and human sexuality. They signaled that if black female bodily integrity were protected—if black women were delivered from the pervasive threat of sexual violence—the women would exercise their sexuality and perform the labors of the body in accordance with Victorian ideals. Their efforts—protection through restraint—represented, however, only one of the tracks along which women resisted, that is, the protectionist response.

Therefore it is important to direct attention to another, less recognized tradition among the period's blues women embraced by the black working class and the poor, what Davis refers to as an "unacknowledged tradition of feminist consciousness in working-class black communities."[113] As it happens:

> The birth of the blues coincided with a period of militant activism by middle-class black women directed at white racists for whom rape was a weapon of terror, and at white employers who routinely used sexual violence as a racialized means of asserting power over their female domestic help.[114]

Davis goes on to ask, "What can we learn from women like Gertrude "Ma" Rainey, Bessie Smith and Billie Holiday that we may not be able to learn from Ida B. Wells, Anna Julia Cooper, and Mary Church Terrell?"[115]

We can learn a great deal. In contrast to the "politics of respectability" and the "culture of dissemblance," blues women spoke out against violations of their bodily integrity and their experiences of sexual and physical violence without downplaying their sexuality. On the contrary they claimed the right to an "outrageous" sexuality. Quoting Daphne Duval Harrison, Davis notes that the women represented "an emerging model for the working-woman—one who is sexually independent, self-sufficient, creative and trendsetting."[116] Creative and trendsetting. In their songs, Davis says, we see "a validation of individual emotional needs and desires."[117] I see this and more. I see a pushback against the tendency to view the realm of sexuality and emotion as lower-order and functional, as only serving the race's higher aims. They called attention as well to the place and necessity of emotional attachments in dignified human life, however unstable or fleeting. As Harrison observes of blues women, "Maybe her man would take her back, maybe not; and maybe she doesn't care if he doesn't"[118]—or better, in the words of Ida Cox's "Wild Woman," "I've got a disposition and a way of my own. When my man starts kicking, I let him find another home."[119] These attitudes prevail over a functionalist view of capacities most closely associated with femininity, only to be harnessed, stabilized, or only exercised in service of the race's higher aims.

The blues women labored to expand discursive horizons regarding black female sexual desire, pleasure, and leisure pursuits, and therefore represent not the protectionist arm of the respectability leaning clubwomen set, but the enhancement arm of the struggle for intimate equality. Davis states that "One of the most obvious ways in which blues lyrics deviated from that era's established popular musical culture was their provocative and pervasive sexual—including homosexual—imagery."[120] They embraced their appetites in the face of black sexual minimalists in the "politics of respectability" set. What is more, they boasted of their sexual prowess and notably did not thematize motherhood.

If Anna Julia Cooper and the clubwomen did valuable work in insisting that black female bodily integrity mattered, that it had to be protected and of presenting a nonhierarchically organized black body for politics, correctly calling attention to the need to the need to devote collective—and not necessarily patriarchal—resources to protecting bodily integrity, blues women provided a vision of what collective enhancement, and not simply protection, of the realm in which the physical, emotional, and sexual needs of the black body are met might engender. I will argue that we should work to bring about what they called for in the present by adapting Martha Nussbaum's elaboration of the capabilities approach.

Famously, blacks failed to secure all they sought in this period. It is critical that we keep the capabilities approach in mind as we consider what collective racial justice requires today, given the failures of this period. I turn to this in chapter 5.

[4]

INTIMATE INJUSTICE, POLITICAL OBLIGATION, AND THE DARK GHETTO

The urban poor should not be demonized, stigmatized or otherwise dehumanized, just as surely as they should not be romanticized. Yet it would be a mistake to think that they should never be morally criticized.

—Tommie Shelby, "Justice, Deviance and the Dark Ghetto"[1]

For although black men suffer under the weight of racial stereotypes that constrict their lives in myriad ways, they also reap material and psychological rewards for perpetuating black patriarchal practices such as street harassment. . . . Just as rape is not about sex, street harassment is not about flirtation or courtship. Both acts are meant to assert male dominance over women in situations where women appear vulnerable.

—Hawley Fogg-Davis, "Theorizing Black Lesbians within Black Feminism: A Critique of Same-Race Street Harassment."[2]

There exists a clear legal framework to reproach sexual harassment and abuse in the home and at work, but when it comes to the streets—all bets are off. This gap isn't because street harassment hurts any less, it's because there hasn't been a solution. Until now . . .

—ihollaback.org

On May 11, 2003 two black men propositioned fifteen-year-old Sakia Gunn and four of her friends at a bus stop in downtown Newark. The black teens were on their way home from a night out in Manhattan. When the young women stated that they were lesbians and rejected the advances, the men attacked them. Valencia Bailey, one of the teens attacked, described what transpired: "The men called, 'Yo shorty come here.' We told them, 'No we're ok. We're not like that. We're gay.'" Chantell Woodridge, another member of the group, reports seeing one of the men choking her sister: "My sister was foaming at the mouth." She also witnessed what next transpired with Gunn. Richard McCullough told her, "Come here." Gunn replied, "No, you're not my father." McCullough grabbed Gunn by the neck and placed a knife to her throat. She fought back, escaping his grasp once before he stabbed her in the chest, killing her.[3]

The events outlined above took place next to a twenty-four-hour police booth that was at the time unmanned, the empty booth a symbol of the absence of state protection for the teens, including the absence of protection for their free sexual expression. The event itself received considerably less national media attention than that of Matthew Shepard, but it sparked several protests, rallies, and vigils in low-income black communities in Newark. Several LGBT groups also formed in the wake of her shooting, including the Newark Pride Alliance and Sakia Gunn Aggressives and Femmes.[4] Two thousand five hundred people attended Gunn's funeral.

Reflecting on the events leading up to Gunn's murder, Hawley Fogg-Davis[5] argued that blacks should not tolerate the same-race street harassment that pervades urban black communities:

> There are specific "oughts" that ought to be taught in black families, schools, churches, and community organizations concerning the treatment of black girls and women within black civic life and black feminists should not equivocate on this. Chief among these "oughts" is for boys and men to understand the psychological and existential harms they inflict when they participate

in a longstanding culture of street harassment, and for black girls and women not to dismiss such harm as trivial.[6]

The problem of gendered public violence is perceived to be so pervasive in inner cities that a growing number of urban social activists have begun to address the disproportionate sexist street harassment they experience. The Brooklyn-based organization Girls for Gender Equity (GGE), for example, has politicized the challenge of affording inner-city girls and young women the same access to public space as boys. Arguing that boys and young men must learn to share the street fairly because it is not exclusively male space, GGE has made sexist street harassment its raison d'être. Suggesting that the focus of police and school officials on the issue of male gang violence leads many young women to conclude that gender-based violence, intimidation, and harassment do not matter to community leaders, GGE places sexist street harassment on a continuum of pervasive public violence that circumscribes girls' movement from home to school and places of leisure. Precisely because such constraints negatively affect girls' psychosocial development, these social-justice activists are campaigning to pressure community members to create conditions in public spaces that foster the healthy development of all children.[7]

In taking up the issue of same-race street harassment, feminist theorists and activists call attention to a raced-gendered dimension of a just society omitted in leading theories of justice. The magnitude and pervasiveness of the practice are not exaggerated in either Fogg-Davis or GGE's accounts. It is a significant problem that community institutions often simply ignore, and calls for acknowledgement represent a significant step in the right direction. Yet in framing the issue as a problem to be addressed in and by the black community through pronouncements from its institutions that can be taken up immediately by individual community members, this approach fails to consider the pervasive effects of racism on everyday life in impoverished urban neighborhoods in the contemporary United

States, and in particular the effects of racism on gendered subject formation. It also fails to consider how any fair assessment of the obligations of blacks must consider historical events and contemporary circumstances that produced and maintain black enclaves in inner cities and survival practices within them. Racist violence, racial discrimination in the practices of banks, mortgage companies, real estate agents, public housing policies, and continuing economic marginalization and constraint have to be taken into account in developing a comprehensive theory of justice for young women here as well as in outlining shorter-term strategies for social change.[8] Black community institutions, which Fogg-Davis correctly identifies as the site of change, must do more than issue "shoulds" to individuals who may or may not possess the capacities necessary to undertake the desired behavior; the institutions must develop strategies that enable nonviolent interactions. Yet institutional racism has bequeathed to black community institutions far greater challenges than those facing institutions within the wider society—particularly when it comes to the issue of public violence. How then can they be expected to meet these greater challenges with significantly fewer resources?

Fogg-Davis and the work of GGE call attention to one among many significant obstacles to "intimate justice" facing women and girls in inner-city black communities. In this chapter, I place the experiences of African American women and girls at the center of analysis in order to demonstrate the defects of conceptions of injustice and political obligation that fail to take race and gender seriously. Using Tommie Shelby's searing account of the impact of institutional racial injustice on civic obligation in the "dark ghetto" as my point of departure, I demonstrate why any comprehensive theory of injustice and the obligations vitiated that by injustice must attend to intimate injustice.[9] I hold that if black women and men are to experience the full benefits of a just society, then we must find means to address barriers to free sexual expression, reproduction, and caregiving, as well as the problems of disproportionate punitive scrutiny, violence, and intimidation across a range of institutions, including institutions regulating reproduction and care, that circumscribe their lives in contemporary U.S. cities. Establishing meaningful intimate justice is every bit as important as economic and political justice; thus, until intimate justice is established, black women do not have the same obligations as those that bind members of the wider society. Also, because Shelby's account ignores the contours of intimate injustice and does not attend to the impact of the dark-ghetto social climate on his subjects' abilities to act and make choices and centers a fully developed tacitly male subject who only acts in economically deprived civic space instead of a developmentally disadvantaged subject who experiences injustice in civic and intimate contexts, he misses serious challenges to blacks' ability to meet the civic obligations that, he holds, remain under conditions of racial injustice in dark ghettos.

GENDERED CONTOURS OF SHELBY'S DARK GHETTO

In "Justice, Deviance, and the Dark Ghetto," Tommie Shelby advances an impressive critique of John Rawls's *A Theory of Justice*.[10] In his now famous formulation, Rawls argues that a just society is characterized by equal liberty, but equal liberty does not necessitate economic equality. Although formal political equality is absolutely essential, differences in economic status are acceptable as long as any economic differences made the worst-off better off than they would otherwise be. In such a "well-ordered" society, each citizen has reciprocal obligations to fellow citizens to uphold existing institutions and respect the rules by which those institutions operate. Many theorists have claimed that the United States roughly approximates Rawls's two principles of justice: the U.S. Constitution guarantees equality before the law, and the capitalist economic system ensures that the poor in this country are far better off than the poor elsewhere. Thus all U.S. citizens are bound to uphold the existing political order. At a time when struggles over civil rights, racism, the Vietnam War, economic inequities, and the Equal Rights Amendment brought millions of citizens into the streets protesting the legitimacy of existing institutions, the adequacy of Rawls's theory of justice and its applicability to the United States were subjects of intensive debate.

In a powerful intervention into these debates, Shelby argues that political and economic conditions in dark ghettos fail to meet Rawlsian standards of justice. Far from providing formal equality and economic opportunity, U.S. political institutions at local, state, and federal levels are riddled with racial bias. African Americans do not possess equal formal political power relative to members of the wider society. They do not have equal access to employment-oriented skill acquisition or equal access to employment itself. They do not experience equal treatment within the criminal justice system. On the contrary, they suffer political and economic marginalization despite Constitutional guarantees of equality under the law, and they are subjected to racially motivated heightened scrutiny and disproportionate police harassment, intimidation, and violence.[11] Data to substantiate such claims are readily available. To take just one example from New York City police "stop and frisk" policies: "In 2009, a record 575,304 people were stopped, 87 percent of whom were Black and Hispanic, while from 2005 to 2008, approximately 80 percent of total stops made were of Blacks and Latinos, who comprise approximately 25 percent and 28 percent of New York City's total population, respectively."[12] In the words of Vincent Warren, executive director of the Center for Constitutional Rights, "2009 was the worst year for stop-and-frisks on record. For many kids, getting stopped by the police while walking home from school has become a normal afterschool activity, and that's tragic."[13] Moreover, although residents of dark ghettos are often in contact with police, they have far less personal security than members of the wider society, as they receive inadequate protection from the state. They are thus subject both to high levels of interpersonal and community violence and to brutality at the hands of the police.[14]

Illuminating the effects of economic marginalization, Shelby draws much-needed attention to the assault on human dignity and the resulting sense of alienation and non-belonging associated with racial/spatial injustice. He conceives blacks' relegation to low- wage, menial jobs within an advanced capitalist, consumerist society as a potent form of economic and political marginalization. He also connects residents' sense of alienation from the wider society to the experience of violence, intimidation, and harassment at the hands of agents of the criminal justice system that blacks, particularly black males, encounter as they move through neighborhood streets. Precisely because of such pervasive inequity, Shelby asserts that low-income inner-city blacks do not have the same obligations as those that bind members of the wider society. They are not obligated, for example, to adhere to the wider society's norms regarding work; they are not required to seek such menial employment as may be available to them. On the contrary, they are justified in seeking economic opportunities within a parallel economy, defined as illicit by society at large. Rather than acquiesce in the dignity-destroying racist economy, Shelby suggests that dark-ghetto residential streets become reasonable workspaces under conditions of injustice.[15] Shelby also defends a sense of self-restoring oppositional or defiant attitude with regard to the wider society's authority figures, its codes of behavior, and its economic and civic norms.

I see Shelby's "Justice, Deviance, and the Dark Ghetto," as an application of his arguments regarding racial solidarity in his *We Who Are Dark: The Philosophical Foundations of Black Solidarity* to a specific location: spatially isolated, politically and economically marginalized black neighborhoods.[16] In the book he argues that blacks must commit to racial solidarity in order to achieve the extension of Rawlsian principles of justice to blacks. The "deviance" he defends among dark-ghetto residents is an expression of what blacks should do until there is Rawlsian justice in these communities.

Although Shelby holds that they may reasonably engage in "deviant" economic and social behavior, that is, behavior that deviates from established social norms, Shelby insists that individual residents must refrain from violent behavior. Additionally, although impoverished blacks do not have the same set of civic obligations that bind people within the wider society, they do have obligations to themselves and to each other. Black inner-city residents retain the duty to strive—with community members and allies in the wider society—for racial justice, which Shelby defines as the complete application of liberal principles of economic and political opportunity across the color line. Noting that the fight for racial justice requires racial solidarity, Shelby suggests that residents may not take part in activities, including interpersonal or civic violence against fellow dark-ghetto residents, which erodes that solidarity. Thus Shelby concurs in Fogg-Davis's prescription that resource-deprived black communities must nonetheless establish codes of conduct that sustain black solidarity and civic life.

I agree with Shelby's assessment of the injustice of dark-ghetto political and economic conditions.[17] Yet his account of the residents of the dark ghetto and the problems they confront leaves much to be desired. All residents seem to be more or less fully developed. He depicts a world of adults and adolescents, all presumably male beings unencumbered by sexual, reproductive, or caring obligations. Like many liberal theorists before him, Shelby's residents do not appear to participate within the society's system of social reproductive cooperation. They manifest no concerns about the needs of the young, the elderly, or even their own daily sustenance. Because this gendered system of social cooperation goes unremarked in Shelby's account of dark-ghetto conditions, there is no mention of the impact that racial bias and overall unfairness, past and present, have on those who assume caregiving responsibilities. In a piece in which spatial isolation is one of the key features of injustice, Shelby devotes no attention to the manifold ways that residential segregation and widely disparate racial geography compounds not only distributive unfairness but also contemporary social reproductive unfairness. Nor does he consider how past and present social reproductive unfairness may affect individual residents' capacities to refrain from violence.

In Shelby's account there seem to be only older and younger male dark-ghetto residents—economic actors all—and police on the street. Each young man is free to and fully capable of choosing his relations, his affiliations, and the nature of each of his discrete interactions each day. In making these choices, he confronts only the options of joining the formal or parallel economy, upholding norms and adhering to nonviolence or turning to deviant economic interactions. He also can decide whether to engage in violence or to refrain from doing so.

As well, Shelby's account of racial constraints, like his discussion of a male-focused parallel economic sector, envisions life on dark-ghetto streets without women. His vision of the inner city as a space of economic actions and transactions ignores other significant racialized systems and constraints that contribute to a sense of alienation and non-belonging—and, indeed, have powerful effects on the cultivation of individual capabilities, including the capacity to choose. When women's lives in the dark ghetto are taken into account, then new terrains of dark-ghetto injustice become visible. When sexual, reproductive, and caring behaviors are taken into account, other key forms of racialized constraint and alienation come into sharp focus.[18] Consider, for example, the institutional bias within the system of child protective services and the constraints that system places on black caregiving and family integrity. This system functions in conjunction with phenomena of racial geography such as spatial mismatch, which creates longer commuting times for dark-ghetto caregivers, which in turn impacts the time that residents are able to devote to caregiving, as well as the quality of caregiving that residents are able to provide. Racist interventions by child protective services and working caretakers' spatial isolation from relatively distant employment centers have a critical impact on the psychological and emotional development of the male (and female) subjects dwelling in the dark ghetto. Racist decisions that remove black children from their families are unjust in and of themselves, the longer commuting times black women must undertake are unjust in and of themselves, but they may also have profound effects on a developing individual's capacity to control violent reactions to inequitable treatment. Lack of attention to the impact of intimate injustice, then, leaves Shelby's theory unable to secure one of his prized objectives—the compliance of resident youths with nonviolent codes of conduct that sustain black solidarity, civic life, and the struggle for racial justice.

Shelby's account also obscures the violence women experience in the course of gendered, non-economic interactions on the street. Women's experience of street harassment helps to bring into focus the fact that much of human behavior within dark-ghetto social space is far less about choice and more a function of social climate. In stark contrast to Shelby's choosing male agent, there is the "thrown" female subject.[19] Black women have little choice but to interact with the residents they meet on the street. They are often compelled to interact with boys and men in the complex social environment of the dark ghetto and risk violence when they do not. In fact, gradations of coercion and constraint circumscribe all interactions between residents and state agents, men and men, men and women, and boys and girls on inner-city streets. This thrownness complicates choice for men and women, boys and girls. As Nikki Jones has noted, the urban environment that young women and girls must navigate and in which they must make decisions about economic and intimate action is riddled with violence.[20] But urban interpersonal violence is not unconnected to the fact that there are few resources available for young men of color to develop nonviolent masculine identities. There is a severe "lack of resources to help young men take on a masculine identity that does not involve physical domination or violence and equally limited resources available to help young women protect themselves from everyday threats of violence in their relationships with boys and men."[21] As Elijah Anderson has demonstrated:

> The code of the streets is actually a cultural adaptation to a profound lack of faith in the police and judicial system—and in others who would champion one's personal security. The police, for instance, are most often viewed as representing the dominant white society and as not caring to protect inner-city residents.

When called, they may not respond, which is one reason many residents feel they must be prepared to take extraordinary measures to defend themselves and their loved ones against those who are inclined to aggression.[22]

Lacking the institutional support that sustains personal security, a black youth may have few options other than to become someone who must constantly be on guard to defend himself, by violence if necessary. Absence of the resources that enable male residents to become nonviolent individuals is yet another dimension of injustice in the dark ghetto.

Recognition that nonviolent behavior is an achievement that depends on particular social conditions and institutions—including the family—indicates that an adequate theory of dark-ghetto justice must take "social climate" into account.[23] To the extent that violent masculine identities themselves stem from racist institutions and practices and inadequate resources within the dark ghetto, then it is unreasonable to expect boys and men to simply refrain from violence. And to the extent that institutional deficiencies stem from racist dynamics in society at large, it does not make sense to impose the obligation to address violence on the black community alone. As well, a comprehensive theory of justice must address gendered developmental patterns in order to address street interactions. Thus, a comprehensive theory of justice must attend to "intimate justice," to sexual practices, reproductive relations, caregiving, and caretaking that shape individual capacities and identities, including "choices" to engage in violent or nonviolent behavior.

In fact, in order to develop a conception of justice adequate to the developmental and other needs of both young women and men in the dark ghetto, we must shift away from an account of dark-ghetto injustice that focuses on the unfair distribution of resources among discrete, fully formed, and relatively unencumbered residents. We must purge the vestiges of atomistic individualism that informs notions of residents who have significant power to choose their interactions and control the nature of those interactions with civic peers and with police. In its place, we need to craft an account of justice that illuminates and addresses the injustice of racialized group-based insecurities that have profound effects on individual subject formation.[24] An adequate theory of justice must engage the risk of violence and how exposure to violence and disproportionate punishment affect not only what resources residents of the dark ghetto can secure, but what developing residents are allowed to do and who they are allowed to become.[25] Rather than positing formal equality as sufficient, justice theorists must attend to and creatively address myriad inequities, noxious practices, and racist institutions that comprise the violent social climate in which subjects live. Through this understanding, an adequate theory of justice will enable subjects to be who they want to be, not simply to have what they might want to have.

Disproportionate risk of violence, exposure to violence, and the ever-present threat of institutional and interpersonal violence and punishment are significant debilitating phenomena within the social environment of the dark ghetto that impair residents' ability to convert such resources as they may secure into political, economic, and social reproductive well-being or functioning.[26] But beyond the use of resources, living in the shadow of violence affects residents' ability "to do and to become" all that they would be in this space, including their ability to live as nonviolent individuals among nonviolent individuals. The impact of this violence on residents' "doings and becomings" demands the attention of justice theorists. For this reason, an adequate theory of justice must be attentive to imbalances over and above inequitable resources. Justice requires dark-ghetto social climate reform.

If we are to succeed in removing the undue constraints facing women and men in intimate and civic space, in the home and on the streets, short-term solutions require that we not rest content with a call for nonviolence and a collective struggle against only political and economic injustice.

INTIMATE INJUSTICE, PAST AND PRESENT

I should note that Shelby's analysis of current dark-ghetto condi-tions is informed by the peculiar racist history and geography of the United States, with its legacy of racialized political and economic subordination and marginalization. But it pays no heed to "the repro-ductive history of African American women [which] has been shaped by coercion, cruelty, and brutality."[27] Shelby includes a brief account of historic conditions of racial injustice—slavery and Jim Crow—but does not comment specifically on the sexual, reproductive, and social reproductive unfairness of racial orders past, including the associ-ated violence and brutality.[28]

The long history of the wider society's failures regarding social reproductive fairness for dark-ghetto residents, which have always disproportionately targeted women, cannot be ignored in any theory of black obligation to one another and to the wider society under con-ditions of racial injustice.

Nor is it possible to relegate injustices in the realm of sexuality, reproduction, and caregiving to the past. Each day women, includ-ing young women and girls, must move through dark-ghetto streets not simply to their places of employment and employment-oriented skill acquisition but also to sexual and reproductive health services; they must navigate a racial geography thoroughly penetrated by child protective services. These services are racially biased, organized more to oversee, constrain, and punish blacks as sexual, reproductive, and caring beings than to assist them. Such reproductive health services as are available may bear more resemblance to population control centers than health care, for example. The foster-care system is also an excellent case in point: as Dorothy Roberts notes, "Many poor African American neighborhoods have high rates of child welfare agency involvement, especially placement of children in foster care."[29] The "racial geography" of child protective services is marked by high levels of contact between social-services agencies and parents, yet few family preservation services are available. Targeted racial bias against African American parents in child removal policy and concentrated involvement of child welfare agencies in African American neighborhoods set the parameters of institutional injustice here. The institutions assigned the task of regulating social reproduction violate principles of fairness in their standard operating procedures, placing burdens on black parents not experienced by other parents in the wider society. Part of the injustice here regards state decisions about what policies to fund, and state preference for punitive disruptive policies (contributing to the "parenting punishment gap") over policies designed to support and reunify families (policies that enable reproductive and relationship capacity), as foster care costs more per child than adequate welfare provision for impoverished black families.[30]

Roberts calls the American foster-care system an apartheid system, designed to deal with black familial problems in disruptive and disabling ways. The charge of apartheid certainly rings true in cities like New York, where three-fourths of children removed from their homes are black, and one in ten children in Central Harlem is in foster care, a rate of child removal experienced by few other poor communities.

> Predominantly Latino Hunts Point, in the Bronx, is even poorer than Central Harlem. The rate of single parenthood in the community is the same (and, in any event, children are no more likely to be abused in single parent homes than in homes with two parents, when the figures are adjusted for family income). But a child is almost twice as likely to be taken from his parents in Central Harlem. One in 19 children is taken in Hunts Point versus almost one in ten in Central Harlem. Compare these data, further, to a poor white community, and there is evidence of discrimination against Blacks and Latinos. In predominantly white Ridgewood and Glendale in Queens, which has about one-half the poverty rate of these two neighborhoods, only 1 in 200 children was in foster care in 1998.[31]

The magnitude of racial bias is astounding, particularly when one considers that the Department of Health and Human Services acknowledges that the overwhelming number of children in foster care are there, not because of abuse, but because of the fairly amorphous category of "neglect." What gets defined as neglect often stems from issues of work–life balance, exacerbated by the distance of the laboring caretaker from employment centers, as a function of spatial mismatch, inadequate child care, and inadequate housing—a problem with clear connections to racial discrimination in American housing markets.

> Out of every 100 children investigated as possible victims of abuse, four are "substantiated" victims of all forms of physical abuse, from the most minor to the most severe, about 2 more are victims of sexual abuse. Many of the rest are false accusations or cases in which a family's poverty has been confused with neglect. . . . Far more common than a child who comes into care because he was beaten are children who come into foster care because the food stamps ran out or because an illness went untreated after parents were kicked off Medicaid or because a single mother trying to stay off welfare could not provide adequate supervision while she worked. . . . Three separate studies since 1996 have found that 30% of America's foster children could be safely in their own homes right now, if their birth parents had safe, affordable housing. A fourth study found that in terms of reunification, even substance abuse is not as important a factor as income or housing in determining whether children will remain with their families.[32]

The National Coalition for Child Protection Reform states that although parents need obvious things like reliable and safe daycare and babysitting, they are offered only foster care.[33] This is decidedly unjust given the history and current patterns of residential segregation and the placement of employment centers in the United States.

Beyond their treatment by social-services agencies, black working caregivers also face major issues pertaining to transportation in dark ghettos. As Edward Soja has documented, transportation policy is structured around the commuting needs of the average white male worker, which differ markedly from the needs of dark-ghetto residents.[34] Black women caregivers are concentrated in inner cities relatively distant from employment centers. They disproportionately rely on public transportation to get to their jobs. Working longer hours to make ends meet than their wider-society counterparts, they then face longer commuting times than wage-earning caretakers within the wider society.[35] The difficult commuting situation, which results from the mismatch between black residential areas and employment sites, unduly burdens residents' capacity to provide care for children. It diminishes the time they are able to spend providing care and may also diminish the quality of the care they provide. Long work days and prolonged commuting times that contribute to physical exhaustion are then coded by the social-services bureaucracy as "neglect," which contributes to the overrepresentation of black children in the foster-care system. Long working hours and long commutes also diminish the time black women can spend with intimate partners and the quality of relationships they forge.

DARK GHETTO INTIMATE OBLIGATIONS

In light of these issues, in approaching the question of intracommunal and societal obligations, the question we must ask is: What must residents of the dark ghetto be required to do for others—for society as a whole and for their neighbors—taking into account the unique political, economic, geographic, and social reproductive features of the dark ghetto?

To Shelby's account of vitiated obligations I add that obligations that are ostensibly founded on fairness regarding reproduction and caring labor are sorely tested in the dark ghetto, given the history of racial injustice in this scheme of social cooperation.[36] In light of these conditions, women who reside in dark ghettos, in particular, are under no obligation to take part in the inequitable system of social reproduction that exists within the wider society.[37]

To Shelby's reasonable and, I think, impressive arguments regarding dark-ghetto residents' political and economic obligation, I add that the biased treatment that residents have long received as sexual, reproductive, and caretaking beings vitiates their obligation to take part in the wider society's unjust system of social-reproductive cooperation, just as it vitiates their obligation to accept the wider society's efforts to structure and coerce this cooperation within dark ghettos. They have no obligation to comply with welfare reform efforts devoted to forcing caretakers into marriage and low-wage service labor, for example.[38]

What "deviant" behaviors can reasonably be defended under such an arrangement? I argue that black women may reasonably adopt an oppositional attitude toward social norms regarding family formation. Indeed, given the history and contemporary practice of family disruption, behavior that deviates widely from the acceptable norms of mainstream society is reasonable. As an apartheid system, child protective services lacks legitimate authority over black households. In cases of child neglect (thought not in cases of abuse, in keeping with Shelby's prohibition on actions that enable violence in these communities), black families should not be required to surrender their children to this system.[39] Black women should not have to submit to racist forms of reproductive health service in their communities and might reasonably adopt self-help techniques.

What specific menial jobs in the formal economy should black women shun? I would venture that black women should shun those jobs directed toward caring labor for the larger society outside the ghetto. Women of the dark ghetto should be encouraged to devote their energies to subverting, not propping up, the racially biased system of reproductive regulation and cooperation.[40]

Regarding black obligations to one another, the problem of sexist street harassment must be addressed explicitly and in concert with increased resource provision from the wider society and creative efforts to transform the hostile social environment. Although they are not responsible for all aspects of the hostile social climate in the dark ghetto, men must think of themselves as part of that social environment. As such, they should seek resources to cultivate capacities that contribute to intimate racial justice. Indeed, they should seek to help end the undue burdens imposed on black women in the realm of sexuality and reproduction in dark ghettos. Black men also have a further obligation, though they must have community support, security, and leadership to help them develop the emotional capacities necessary to fulfill this duty. With appropriate resources and support, black men must provide supportive, regenerative contexts for black female intimate life, regenerative contexts in which black women are free to exercise their sexual and reproductive capacities in an expansive way in accordance with the conditions of justice outlined in the capability approach. They are, with sufficient community support, not only obligated to refrain from violence, harassment, and intimidation, but must intervene to empower women. Within a context of systemic transformation of the social environment, the regenerative strategies that are necessary for realizing intimate racial justice presuppose strong black institutional commitments—collective endeavors—to address how men and boys interact with women and girls in ghetto streets.

SITUATING STREET HARASSMENT IN RELATION TO INTIMATE JUSTICE

Women in dark ghettos face systematic injustice in their endeavors to live as sexual, reproductive, and caretaking beings. As elaborated above, the spatial mismatch between home and workplace, low wages, biased reproductive health services, and high rates of disruptive child welfare involvement drastically curtail their capacities to act. Because male residents of the dark ghetto also face unique burdens associated with the racialized social climate, they exercise constrained choices—and the levels of constraint are not fully acknowledged in Shelby's

account.[41] But constrained choice is compatible with disparate gendered power that can add to the undue burdens and constraints upon
women's lives in dark ghettos. In this sense, black male residents of
the dark ghetto can make choices to exacerbate or alleviate women's
burdens.[42] The current security provision regime and the prevailing
economic and political institutions constrain the formal political
power and economic action of black males, yet black men themselves
are empowered by this racist-patriarchal system to constrain or dominate the civic and intimate lives of women and girls. Subject formation in the dark ghetto is fraught, and much more needs to be done
to transform the social climate from thoroughly oppressive to supportive of full human development and functioning. However, particularly under these conditions of constrained choice, black men and
boys must be provided resources to enhance their supportiveness of
black women.[43] In addition to being a site where blacks' overall sense
of (non-)belonging within the wider society is cultivated and urban
injustice is enacted, the street is a critical space of gender subordination.[44] The street is a place where police assert undue power over
young black men, relying upon the pervasive notion that young black
men are criminals to sustain their actions. Through such practices,
police, aided and abetted by the wider society, have undue power to
determine *what* (as opposed to *who*) young black men are—criminals
rather than youth, for example. But the street is also a significant
space where men exercise undue power over women and girls. Same-
race street harassment accords black men and boys undue power to
determine what young women and girls are, constricting their freedom to decide who they are and what they will do and be. Men and
boys wield this power by initiating sexualized interactions to which
girls must respond or risk violence. In the context of the hostile social
climate of the dark ghetto, supported and unchecked by patriarchal
conditions in the community and the wider society, street harassment constrains young women's and girls' endeavors to create their
own visions and plans for their sexual and reproductive lives. It can
affect their decisions about the prominence of their sexuality relative to other dimensions of their lives and life plans. It can pressure

them to prioritize sexuality over school or sports or their relations with other girls or, at a later point, their careers. It may accord sexual activity undue weight across all stages of their lives, bringing it into focus too soon, too often, and in objectifying ways that fail to respect the humanity and subjectivity of young women and girls.

The street is a space where men and boys often disrupt a young woman's ability to decide for herself the relative priority to assign to sexual activity. Harassing encounters may also pressure young women toward particular sexual partners they might not choose under other circumstances. Thus the street may shape black women's sense of belonging and non-belonging to the community and the wider society quite differently from their male counterparts. Street harassment may teach women and girls that neither the black community nor the wider society is committed to treating them fairly, to supporting and providing protection for all aspects of their lives, including their intimate lives. Street harassment disempowers female residents of the dark ghetto relative to their male counterparts and disadvantages them relative to privileged women in the wider society, whose safety and security are more likely to receive police protection.

Intimate racial justice demands that men never add to the undue burdens black women face, and requires them to refrain from sexualizing and objectifying women in ways that constrain their self-determination. In light of black women's historic and contemporary experience of intimate violence, black men have a particular obligation not to replicate this form of violence. From the point of view of intimate racial justice, black men and boys should actively intervene to empower women, helping them to exercise their sexual and reproductive capacities in the truly human way that has been denied them for much of our nation's history. But black men cannot fulfill these obligations alone. They require resources from the wider community to transform the hostile climate and secure their safety and security, as well as support from black community-based organizations to redress the debilitating effects of the dark ghetto.

INTIMATE JUSTICE

The world of possessive individualism projected from such a skewed conception about human society is a world in which the only players who matter are adult white men, competing with one another and adjudicating their disputes with contracts. Love, trust, friendship, art, invention—all are irrelevant to instrumental agreements about the distribution of property.[1]

In *Arrested Justice: Black Women, Violence, and America's Prison Nation*, Beth Richie uses a series of stories to illustrate black women's disproportionate experience of intimate-partner violence, household violence (that is, the violence women experience at the hands of those who share their household but with whom they are not romantically involved), bystander violence, sexual assault and sexual aggression from community members, and the sexual exploitation and aggression they experience in police and state custody within what she calls America's "prison nation," where police violence is the last on a continuum of physical and sexual violence black women experience at the hands of men. It is worth pausing to note here that - in a contemporary context in which police violence now commands significant mainstream attention - that racial profiling by the police often takes gender specific forms that often lead to sexual assault.[2]

Richie, for example, relates the story of the brutal rape of a Haitian American woman in the Dunbar Village Housing projects, as well as the gang rape of a seven-year-old girl in Trenton, New Jersey. She tells the story of a teenager whose experience of household violence led her to seek shelter with an older man who became an abusive pimp she eventually escaped, but was coerced into killing by the next man with whom she found shelter who, too, became her pimp. (In her reflections on this case she notes that black women's experiences of intimate-partner violence can often look more like human trafficking than more conservative narratives of such violence, which makes conservative models of intimate-partner violence, designed around the experiences of middle-class suburban white women, inadequate to address their needs.) She presents the story of the eleven black women killed by Cleveland-area serial killer Anthony Sowell, their missing-person cases never adequately investigated; of a ninety-two-year-old grandmother killed when police stormed her house in Atlanta, Georgia; of a sixteen-year-old pregnant woman, killed at a bus stop by her thirty-two-year-old foster brother who had been given custody of her when her mother died and with whom—as welfare officials suspected but failed to intervene—she had been having sex, a possible motivation for the murder. Given her age, whether consensual or coerced, it was statutory rape. She tells the story of the New Jersey Four, four lesbian women who were sexually propositioned, followed, and assaulted by a man, and then arrested and served time when their attacker was injured in the course of their efforts (and the efforts of two white men who intervened) to defend themselves. The white men were never interviewed or charged.

Richie's considerable examination of interpersonal, community, and state-sponsored violence against black women leaves her to conclude the following:

> It is not an overstatement to suggest that in the same ways that women are denied power in the relational and domestic spheres, the community embraces a set of dynamics that conspire to foster an environment where individual men can use physical and sexual violence against Black women with few real or long-term consequences. Black community members tolerate direct physical assaults, sexual abuse and aggression, emotional manipulation, and social alienation of Black women.[3]

Richie does not limit her critique to black community members; she also critiques the mainstream anti-gender-based violence movement for its evolving conservatism and its preferential way of mobilizing resources to protect middle-class white women:

> While the anti-violence movement has evolved into a highly organized set of formal responses to the problem of violence against women that has led to an increase in safety for *some* women, this progress has not benefited all women equally. As the work has evolved, the more radical and transformative dimensions of the movement's initial goal—to end violence against women and gender-based oppression in the broader spheres of their lives—was diminished. Today, as the broader political discussion about crime, violence and justice is more conservative, a number of women in positions of power within the anti-violence movement made a series of strategic decisions, moving to work inside the system rather than against it. Subsequently, Black women and other women of color, lesbians, immigrant women, human rights activists, women involved in prostitution, and outspoken survivors of battering and rape continue—30 years later—to find themselves in conflict with other leaders in the anti-violence movement.[4]

While much of the work in previous chapters focuses on history, Richie's work paints a picture of contemporary conditions in black communities. And while Richie rightly calls attention to the failings of community members and activists regarding the violence and gross violations of bodily integrity that black women disproportionately experience today, political theorists must note that these groups would only be stepping in to do a job that the wider political community has long refused to do—and notably a job that political community has done far better for others. It is with Richie's work in mind as well, as the systemic sexual, reproductive, and caretaking violence and terrorism outlined in earlier chapters, that I intervene in a debate between Tommie Shelby and Charles Mills regarding what is necessary to establish racial justice.

WHAT RACIAL JUSTICE DEMANDS

Shelby and Mills look to social-contract theory both to evaluate past racial injustice and to determine what corrective racial justice for blacks might require beyond the standard set of liberal political rights and equality before the law. While they do not share the preoccupations of classical social-contract theory—like their Afro-Modern antecedents they are concerned with outlining and addressing the legacy of American racial domination—they are persuaded by social-contract theory's commitment to creating sociopolitical institutions that reflect human moral equality.

I am convinced by much on offer from each theorist – among many things in particular Shelby's attention to the geography of racial injustice and Mills' insistence that racial justice necessitates correcting for intergenerational white opportunity hoarding – but the solutions they propose for mitigating the impact of past racial justice fail to address all that blacks, and in particular black women and those who have and would today undertake the labors necessary to sustain black life, have suffered, the particular ways in which they have been exploited under racial domination. The solutions they propose are therefore best suited to securing justice for adult black men and those who would not participate in meeting the physical and emotional needs of the black body. This may not come as a surprise as feminists have long argued that an adult male body stands at the center of the social contract theory worldview. If corrective racial justice is simply about blacks receiving what they are due in light of historical racial injustice, we cannot fail to ask what black women and children (and therefore all blacks) are due after centuries of state facilitated and even state sponsored violations of black female bodily integrity, state sanctioned neglect and diminution of black bodily health, including reproductive health, as well as disabling intervention into and an overall failure to support the realm in which the physical and emotional needs of the black body are ment, that is the black intimate sphere. We must ask what black women and children are due from a body politic that came together to diminish blacks' capacities for healthy reproduction and caretaking, to diminish their capacity to care for their young, their sick and their elderly and a body politic that came together to enable white reproduction, caretaking and emotional development, redistributing the physical and emotional benefits of black caring labor to white bodies.

Mills critiques what he sees as the conflation of racial and economic injustice in Shelby's corrective racial justice proposal. I think that it is productive to think of this conflation as Shelby's problematic "embodiment" of corrective racial justice. That is, one might see, in the thinker's focus on economic maldistribution, him singling capacities of the black body that have mattered most, a part of the black body that has mattered most, for protection and enhancement going forward. His concern with economic redistribution demonstrates the most concern for the black body's hands – with how black hands have been misused and even underused, by turns exploited and marginalized – under racial domination. He is most concerned with ensuring that black hands are properly occupied going forward.

That said, Shelby's adaptation of Rawls is laudably "spatialized." Critical geographer and spatial justice theorist Edward Soja states that justice, however it may be defined, has a consequential geography, a spatial expression to which we must attend.[5] Soja goes on to say that Rawls is inattentive to space and presents a problematically aspatial conception of justice. Shelby, by contrast, is attentive to the spatal consequences of racial injustice—he is aware, for example, that blacks' physical distance from employment opportunity matters, and of how even giving an address from an undesirable neighborhood on an employment application can disadvantage blacks who seek employment. Shelby is aware that when it comes to race, space matters, that racial injustice has involved what Soja calls "spatial fixes" that must be addressed in the present. That said, however, our "spatial fixes" will not be the same. Shelby's conception of justice suggests what I see as a far too limited set of geographic consequences.

For his part, one of Mills most persuasive arguemnts is that corrective racial justice must attend to intergenerational white "opportunity hoarding," yet in his elaboration of how whites have done so he focuses on how whites have hoarded positions of advantage in civic life, and therefore does little to correct Shelby's problematic embodiment of racial justice.

I would argue that the two thinkers' sustained engagement with Rawls, whose theory of justice is most concerned with establishing fairness with regard to subejcts' abilities to exercise control over political and material environment and considerably less, if at all concerned with ensuring fainriness in the realm in which the subjects' physical and emotional needs are met, does little to help matters. Feminists, for example, have critiqued Rawls's reluctance to intervene in the family. He tends, Martha Nussbaum says, to ascribe to that institution—and I would add the bodily capacities, labors and activities most closely associated with it—a quasi-natural status. Rawls, she says, by turns conceived of the family as either a natural institution or as a voluntary association when it is, in fact, neither. Furthermore, he tends to begin his analysis from the standpoint of the limits of intervention into the institution and not from the stronger position of what interventions justice most urgently demanded. Nussbuam argues that he should have taken a different approach:

> If instead he had recognized the foundational character of states' presence in the family he might have granted that it makes good sense for principles of justice to recognize and favor whatever units do the job of the family in a way that is compatible with political justice.[6]

It is impossible to put into words the foundational character of the state's presence in this realm for blacks.

Nussbaum also critiques the broader contractarian tendency to regard society as primarily a system of competitive cooperation aimed at generating mutual advantage and therefore emphasizing human capacities for competitive cooperation while deemphasizing other human capacities and suspiciously those most often exercised by women, as well as deemphasizing men's own long period's of dependency. She critiques, as well, the view of what is most important

about our humanity, our embodied existence, underlying this emphasis, the contractarian tendency to value certain aspects of the person
above others and to hold them in opposition to lower parts of the
self. It is worth considering her critique at length. Nussbaum writes:

> In short, the case of people with mental disabilities proves very
> revealing for the entire structure of Rawls's contract doctrine
> and, more generally, for the project of basing principles of justice
> on reciprocity between rough equals who are imagined as joining
> together to reap mutual benefit. Despite the moral elements that
> go very deep in Rawls's theory—and in a sense, also, because of
> them, or the particular Kantian shape they take—Rawls cannot
> altogether outstrip the particular limitations of the contract
> doctrine, which derive from its basic picture of why people live
> together and what the hope to gain therefrom . . .[7]

Nussbaum goes on to offer her alternative:

> Thus the capabilities approach feels free to use a political concep-
> tion of the person that views the person, with Aristotle, as a po-
> litical and social animal, who seeks a good that is social through
> and through, and who shares complex ends with others, at many
> levels. The good of others is not just a constraint on this person's
> pursuit of her own good, it is a *part of her good*. She leaves the
> state of nature not because it is more advantageous in self-in-
> terested terms to make a deal with others, but because she can't
> imagine being whole in an existence without shared ends and a
> shared life.[8]

She continues:

> The second fundamental departure pertains to the notion of dig-
> nity, and thus to Rawls's Kantian contractarianism, which makes
> a notion of dignity basic. Unlike Kant, the capabilities approach
> does not contrast the humanity of human beings with their

animality. It sees the two as thoroughly unified. Taking its cue from Aristotle's notion of the human being as a "political animal," and from Marx's idea that the human being is a creature "in need of a plurality of life-activities," it sees the rational as simply one aspect of the animal, and, at that, not the only one that is pertinent to a notion of truly human functioning. Truly human functioning is animal through and through, and what makes for the specifically human dignity of this functioning is the combination of practical reasoning and sociability that infuses it. . .And bodily need, including the need for care, is a feature of our rationality and our sociability, it is one aspect of our dignity, then, rather than something to be contrasted with it.

Thus, in the design of the political conception of the person out of which basic political principles grow, we build in an acknowledgement that we are needy temporal animal beings who begin as babies and end, often, in other forms of dependency. We draw attention to these vulnerabilities, insisting that rationality and sociability are themselves temporal, with growth, maturity, and (if time permits) decline. The kind of sociability that is fully human includes symmetrical relations (such as those that are central for Rawls), but also relations of more or less extreme asymmetry; we insist that the asymmetrical relations can still contain reciprocity and truly human functioning.[9]

Finally she says:

We can now connect the two fundamental departures from contractarianism, by saying that this new conception of what is dignified and worthy in the human being supports the departure from Rawlsian circumstances of justice. Justice does not begin with the idea that we have something to gain from bargaining together. We have a claim to support based on justice in the dignity of our human need itself. Society is held together by a wide range of attachments, and concerns, only some of which involve productivity. Productivity is necessary, and even good, but it is not the main end of life.[10]

An important part of Nussbaum's critique of contractarianism concerns what it emphasizes about what we are, what is important about our embodied existence and why and how we come together based on this vision of who we are and what is most important about us.

So too with corrective racial justice; we cannot construct an adequate picture of all that blacks have been denied and then use this picture to build an adequate conception of what corrective racial justice demands, by thinking of the black body as a rational locus of competitive cooperation alone. Mills, for example, when he attempts to bring an account of the experiences of black women into his critique of the mainstream contract, focuses on how black women have been disadvantaged as potential cooperators, which, again, is true but incomplete. Instead of accepting the contractarian premise of society, I follow Nussbaum and call attention to the fact that black society is composed of individuals who are both capable of cooperating but who also live through long periods of dependency where others—traditionally and today most often women—would tend to their biological lives, health and physical and emotional needs. I would add, however, that we must couple this with Shelby's attention to the spatiality of racial injustice. We must couple this view of society, as well, with an understanding, deeply influenced by Mills' understanding of what corrective racial justice must address, that is, with an eye towards correcting for how blacks have been disadvantaged and whites advantaged historically. On this view, blacks are disadvantaged not only as potential cooperators, but also as beings who should be afforded bodily integrity as part of securing a dignified life, who would form emotional attachments to others, reproduce, give and receive care. I would suggest, then, that instead of moving forward to establish principles of justice designed to correct for failures regarding competitive cooerpation alone we endeavor instead to correct for all the ways the white body (male nad female) as been advantaged over the black body by racial domination.

Further, given the critiques of Carol Pateman, Moira Gatens, and others regarding the tendency to create political communities with the specific aim of enhancing the capacities of male bodies in mind, it is my argument that Nussbaum provides the best way to "embody" corrective racial justice.

Solutions of the kind Shelby and Mills propose for redistributing economic and socially advantageous positions may help blacks a great deal, but they are incomplete because they provide no redress for the intimate racial injustice felt most acutely by black women and those who have labored and would labor to meet the physical and emotional needs of the black body; perhaps more importantly and tragically, they fail to provide solutions adequate to address the significant racial disadvantages that black women experience today.

I hold that Nussbaum's elaboration of the capabilities approach, complete with its ten central capabilities, which she presents as discrete *and* nonhierarchically ordered, provides a better guide for thinking about historic white opportunity hoarding and for constructing just racial geographies in the present. The approach would help to ensure that corrective racial justice contains far more than the "minor insets" for women, if any are included at all, that Gatens discerns in the modern state.

Nussbaum outlines ten discrete, central capabilities – where capabilities are a combination of "personal abilities alongside the politica, social and economic environment" that community members must have the ability to exericise [11] She goes on to say, "I argue that failure to secure these for citizens is a particularly grave violation of basic justice since these entitilements are held to be implicit in the very notion of human dignity and a life that is worthy of the dignity of the human being."[12] They are 1) Life, 2) Bodily Health 3) Bodily Integrity, 4) Senses, Imagination and Thought, 5) Emotion, 6) Practical Reason, 7) Affiliation, 8) Other Species, 9) Play and 10) Control Over One's Environment (including One's Political and Material Environment).

Nussbaum defines the capability of Life as "Being able to live to the end of a human life of normal length; not dying prematurely, or before one's life is so reduced as to not be worth living."[13] She defines the capability of Bodily Health as "Being able to have good health, including reproductive health; to be adequately nourished; to have adequate shelter." Of Bodily Integrity, Nussbaum says that it entails, "Being able to move freely from place to place, to be secure against violence; having opportunities for sexual satisfaction and for choice in matters of reproduction."[14] She defines the capability of emotion as "Being able to have attachments to things and people outside ourselves; to love those who love and care for us, to grieve at their absence; in general, to love, to grieve, to experience longing, gratitude and justified anger."[15] She holds that in order to be afforded equal concern and respect community members must be able to have attachments to things outside themselves and not have their "emotional development blighted by fear and anxiety."[16]

I suggest the turn to Nussbaum for several reasons, in addition to its fuller account of who we are, what is valuable about us and why we come together. First, the approach notably conceives of each capability as equal and discrete, and therefore ensures that capabilities that have been less socially valued   including the capabilities that are most closely associated with the female body and the material labor that falls to women—do not fall victim to traditional hierarchical conceptions of our body and its capacities in efforts to instantiate equal concern and respect. It helps to guard against constructing corrective racial justice projects that take the black male body as our tacit guide and working simpy to enhance the capacities of the black body most closely associated with men. The approach would devote equal resources to ensuring bodily integrity and ending any community member's disproportionate experience of sexual assault as it would to ending any disadvantage they might face regarding employment. Because the approach conceives of each capability as both discrete and equal—each as worthy of targeted intervention for its own sake—if we follow her approach we are not likely to presume, for example, that once blacks are able to exercise effective control over their political and material environments, their bodily health, bodily integrity, and emotional development will be secured automatically. Additionally, Nussbaum does more than simply proclaim women's negative rights to freedom from sexual assault. She expressly advocates that communities devote positive liberty–style resources to supporting women's reproductive health, sexual satisfaction, genuine and effective reproductive choice, and freedom from intimate-partner violence, sexual harassment, and assault—all things black women have been denied and continue to be denied under racial domination.

Nussbaum provides a better model for evaluating what blacks have been denied under racial domination, including the support, protection, and enhancement of those things to which it has traditionally fallen to women to tend, as well as for the protection and enhancement given to white efforts to exert control over the material and political environment, which are most central to Rawls's, Shelby's, and Mills's concerns. Without such a model, the legacy of black intimate disadvantage will remain insufficiently addressed in projects that, not unsurprisingly, fail to meet the contemporary needs of many black women and children. Far too many among them reside in severely under-resourced communities where women are more likely to experience brutal violations of their bodily integrity and have little or no enabling aid, or worse, encounter disabling intervention regarding their reproductive and caretaking efforts.

It is Nussbaum's far better embodied approach, then, that is best equipped to be adapted to address the harms that the black body has suffered, that blacks have suffered as men and women, as cooperators and caretakers, as beings who require care and who would form emotional attachments to others, reproduce, and tend to the physical and emotional needs of the body. Critically for black women, I will repeat, it is Nussbaum's approach that places black bodily integrity (as well as blacks' ability to form emotional attachments to partners, dependents, and intimates) on equal footing with the ability of blacks to control their material and political environments in securing equal concern and respect. In order to better account for all the ways in which blacks have been disadvantaged, to be "embodied" in a way that better meets the needs of contemporary blacks, corrective racial justice should be guided by the approach Nussbaum advances and the understanding that the full range of the body's capacities need to be enhanced within political communities.

Second, the approach does not naturalize any of the body's capabilities and therefore would afford them more than negative liberty alone so that they might be realized. So, in addition to expliclty naming bodily integrity as part of what political communities are tasked with affording members—and therefore being expressly concerned with mitigating the threats those with feminine embodiment disproportionately face in society including sexual assault and harassment—the approach also calls attention to the positive support necessary to afford such integrity. Black women will certainly require far greater resources to secure their bodily integrity, but Nussaum allows for this, as she states that those who require greater resources to get above a capability threshold because of historic marginalization and discrimination must be given said help. The approach, then, is particularly adaptable to corrective racial justice projects and is in line with the spirit of Mills' call to correct for white opportunity hoarding.

Furthermore, Nussbaum is also laudably aware that capabilities such as bodily integrity can be diminished by more than formal discrimination and outright violence—by laws that exclude black women from the definition of rape, by slave masters, abusive partners, savage experimental gynecologists and the kinds of targeted population control measures that are often discredited once activists bring them to light. She is aware that said integrity can be diminished by diffuse, non-agent originated and even internalized phenomena of the kind to which Hirschmann draws attention. Her approach is attentive to the behavior modifying "fear and anxiety" that arises in contexts where violations of bodily integrity go unpunished. Both her developmental, non-natural and contextual understanding of capabilities and her understanding of how capabilities can be diminished by more than formal inequality and outright violence help to illuminate the severity of the denial of black female bodily integrity throughout American history. Sexual assault within the Jim Crow era was pervasive, but not total, yet from the vantage point of the capability approach all black women in the Jim Crow era through the Joan Little case (a case which arguably marked the end of the social norm that black women were beings who did not have to be afforded bodily integrity) who lived in the climate of fear and anxiety occasioned by the ever present threat of these unpunsied attacks and who lived absent support and proection for bodily integrity saw this capability diminished. From the vantage point of the capabilities approach black women have never been afforded such integrity, thus corrective compensation must be sought for all.

In light of the above, again, I would jettison neither Mills nor Shelby's insights but instead bring them together with Nussbaum's approach and the always only potentially and never naturally, plurally capable individual at the center of her approach. With regard to Mills, I would simply extend the list of opportunities whites have hoarded with explicit reference to Nussbaum's list and then endeavor to correct for how whites have hoarded enabling protection and support for the capabilities of Life, Bodily Health, Bodily Integrity and Emotion, so that blacks are given greater help and resources in getting above these capability thresholds going forward. I would then turn to the matter of what intersectional spatial fixes—in addition to necessary interventions at the level of discourse and the meanings assigned to black bodies, male and female—might be employed in giving blacks the greater help they need in order to get above capability thresholds. Finally, heeding Soja's arguments regarding the importance of the geography of justice and his caution that we attend to "how space is actively involved in generating and sustaining inequality, injustice, economic exploitation, racism, sexism and other forms of oppression and discrimination"[17] and as part of an effort to take Hirschmann's concerns regarding the relationship between context and women's freedom seriously, I would argue that we must attend to space and even endeavor to think intersectionally about the built environment in order to bring about intimate racial justice. If blacks are to be afforded corrective intimate racial justice, black geography must change. The geography that results from implementing corrective racial justice has to contain enabling institutions for reproductive healthcare, but must also include design that facilitates black women's movement through space to these enabling institutions they require and does not function to facilitate the transfer of black caring labor to benefit white bodies. It requires a built environment that facilitates equal use of public space among, blacks and whites, men and women, for example. It would require secure, well lit, public transportation centers built on the model of universal design and not only with an eye for use by the able bodied adult male who is not transporting dependents. Here, I think, we should consider intersectional modifications to the insights of spatial feminists.

Bringing Nussbaum, Shelby and Mills together helps us to see the necessity, within a corrective racial justice project, of posing questions the latter two thinkers leave problematically unposed, such as, "What, beyond the far too belated extension of formal rights (and the much later, again if at all, extension of societal norms) against violations of bodily integrity do black women require so that they are no longer disadvantaged with regard to bodily integrity relative to white women? I would then ask, what specific changes to the built environment does ending this disadvantage require?

REPAIRING THE RACIAL CONTRACT NOW! AND THEN?: RAWLS AND RACIAL JUSTICE

Shelby holds that if fair equality of opportunity truly governed the distribution of income, wealth, and positions of social advantage in our society, then racial justice could be achieved. Rawls's principle of fair equality of opportunity, he says, "addresses one of the most urgent concerns of the least favored races, namely to ensure that their life prospects are not unfairly diminished by the economic inequalities that have been created by a history of racism."[18] He goes on to say that a society that truly guaranteed equality of opportunity for all "would remove many of the socioeconomic burdens that racial minorities shoulder because of the history of racial domination."[19] Shelby outlines a preliminary sketch of what this might look like:

> While I am not sure what set of institutional reforms would be required to realize the principle of equality of opportunity in the United States, it seems clear that it would require, at a minimum, considerable redistribution of wealth, the expansion of educational and employment opportunities and aggressive measures to address discrimination in employment, housing and lending.[20]

Mills, too, believes that "social contract theory can indeed be helpful in theorizing issues of racial justice."[21] He also agrees with Shelby that a major goal of racial justice is to "reduce as far as possible the legacy of racial disadvantage."[22] The contract tradition's attractiveness for him lies in its efforts to create sociopolitical institutions that reflect human moral equality, but he argues that only a modified form of the contract can truly address the needs of groups like blacks who have long been excluded from the sociopolitical structure founded on the moral equality of all white men. He says of social-contract theory generally:

> The contract idea epitomized the birth of a European modernity that challenged patriarchalist and absolutist sociopolitical structures on a foundation of the moral equality of all (white) men. What it does not, of course, capture is the dark side of modernity, the imposition of "absolutist" sociopolitical structures on morally inferior non-Europeans.[23]

With reference to Rawls in particular he argues that, instead of start-ing from a framework that asks what political institutions morally equal persons would accept in Rawls's original position, theorists should start with the reality of exclusion and inequality, where op-pression is normative.[24] An unmodified approach is ineffective be-cause "[t]he mainstream contract takes moral equality as substan-tially recognized and achieved and then asks what kind of polity would be voluntarily created by equal contractors."[25] Mills says that in reality the question for nonwhite men is: what happens when a state and its laws are imposed on them as unequals who are excluded from the contract and—importantly—"what measures of justice would be required to correct for that historic imposition of conquest, expropriation and slavery."[26] Mills outlines his proposed changes to the Rawlsian original position as follows:

> Behind the veil, it would no longer be a matter of choosing self-interestedly, under conditions of ignorance of one's race, an ideal polity, for obviously a nondiscriminatory polity will be the preferred choice. But as agreed, this is not enough to guide us in determining what corrective justice now requires in a polity whose basic structure has been founded on systemic discrimina-tion and racial exploitation. The thought-experiment here would be to imagine what one would prudentially choose to correct for the disadvantage of being born a member of the subordinated race in such a polity.[27]

Mills critiques Shelby's deployment of fair equality of opportunity to bring about racial justice for several reasons. Among the most inter-esting is his criticism of Shelby's deployment of fair equality of oppor-tunity because Rawls developed the principle to mitigate economic disadvantage, which Mills holds is significantly different from racial disadvantage as to make its use ineffective. Racial disadvantage, he says, is not limited to economic disadvantage but also includes a lack of political standing and insufficient consideration of black interests.

Furthermore, he says, the distributive impact of racial disadvantage cannot be conflated with simple class-based disadvantage and a principle designed to address the former must grapple with the intergenerational white advantage in competition for resources and positions of social advantage so that whites are not advantaged in present day competition for positions of social advantage because of this history.

Mills points out that Rawls outlines three conditions where persons might be denied equality of opportunity for positions of social advantage: formal discrimination; fewer natural assets overall, such as mental and physical disability; and class-based disadvantage that renders persons unable to acquire necessary skills for positions of social advantage. But Mills states that there are four. He argues that justice theorists need a fourth category of disadvantage in competition for positions of social advantage that covers "the history of inherited advantages that come from systemic and intergenerational racial exploitation . . . a fourth category to cover these cases of white 'opportunity hoarding.'"[28] He defines opportunity hoarding as a phenomenon in which "whites have illicit advantage that comes about through the inherited legacy of past discriminatory practices sanctioned by law and/or custom."[29] There must therefore be a procedure "so that whites are not unfairly advantaged in competition for positions of social advantage" because of intergenerational racial exploitation.[30]

While there are many avenues to explore regarding their disagreements and the demands of corrective racial justice, I am particularly persuaded by Mills's claim that corrective racial justice must address the phenomenon of white opportunity hoarding. I want to point out, however, that in focusing his own remarks on how whites have hoarded positions of social advantage, he follows Shelby in emphasizing the "work of the hands" and the advantages that have in fact accrued to whites and white bodies on one side of the public/private divide.

I should note that Mills cannot be accused of ignoring gender, gender relations, and patriarchy within his understanding of racial domination. Mills has acknowledged his debt to thinkers like Carole

Pateman; he also draws on a genuinely impressive range of black feminist scholarship in his discussion of gender relations within the "contract of breach." He acknowledges, for example, the place of patriarchy in the struggle against racial domination:

> Thus the struggle for black "manhood"—think of the celebrated placard carried by black demonstrators in the United States in the 1950s and 1960s, "I AM A Man"—usually meant inter alia, the struggle for the restoration of the full range of nonwhite masculine gender privileges taken away by racial patriarchy, an end to the racial subordination of black men as mere subcontractors rather than fully and equally privileged male contractors.[31]

All very true.

What I am saying instead is in order to bring about comprehensive racial justice and specifically to address the deamnds of intimate racial justice we must explicity expand the account of intergenerational white opportunity hoarding we are seeking to correct, to include how whites have been advantaged and blacks disadvantaged regarding bodily security, bodily integrity, and performance of the material labor that typically falls to women, the labor necessary to produce and sustain life. Corrective racial justice cannot naturalize bodily integrity or the labor of the body, which is what it will tend to do if thinkers focus on how blacks were denied equal opportunities to engage in competitive cooperation alone while ignoring how they were disadvantaged as caregivers and dependents.

Part of the problem can be linked to the vision of the body at the center of the contract project, complete with ideas regarding its capacities, its needs, and what constitute its most significant threats, which has long been the subject of feminist critique. I want to suggest that instead we build a corrective racial justice project that seeks to correct for intergenerational white opportunity hoarding based on the body and its capacities, as is on offer in Nussbaum's elaboration of the capabilities approach, with a focus on how we can restructure the built environment and black space as important aspects of the context in which blacks act to fully protect and enable the black body.

HOARDING "THE HELP": THE INTIMATE DIMENSIONS OF RACIAL DISADVANTAGE

Mills calls for a procedure "so that whites are not unfairly advantaged in competition for positions of social advantage" because of inter-generational racial exploitation.[32] But we must go beyond interven-tion to benefit the work of the hands to benefit the black body—all black bodies—and create enabling institutions that intervene to cor-rect for this legacy.

Bringing Mills's insistence that corrective racial justice ad-dress intergenerational white opportunity hoarding together with Nussbaum's elaboration of the ten central capabilities makes ap-parent other hoarding phenomena, revealing a variety of other ways in which racial domination has allowed whites to hoard posi-tive liberty–style support and protection. This is the case because of her developmental and not naturalized conception of our cen-tral capabilities, which require positive liberty–style support for their exercise, as well as the better recognition, in Nussbaum's ap-proach, of the work women disproportionately perform to sustain life, health, and emotional attachment, and explicit recognition of women's own bodily needs and the most significant threats to their bodies. In truth, in bringing them together we bring together Mills's insistence regarding what corrective racial justice demands with a broader view of what we ultimately are, what we must do to sustain ourselves and what is valuable about our embodied existence. When we make it explicit that none of these capabilities are natural and all require the support of the political community for their realization, it becomes apparent that racial domination has allowed whites to hoard that help. This hoarding afforded whites greater opportunities to exercise the capabilities of Life, Bodily Health, Bodily Integrity, and Emotion in a way that must also be addressed in any theory of corrective racial justice. Bringing Mills and Nussbaum creates a host of important new questions: what, for example, beyond formal legal rights and protections, is now necessary to correct for blacks being so long denied opportunities to live to the end of a normal life, denied opportunities for bodily health and bodily integrity, and denied opportunities to form strong emotional attachments to others, when whites have effectively hoarded opportunities to exercise these capabilities?

Whites have not only been advantaged with regard to positions of social advantage; other important aspects of white advantage concern aspects of the body and human life, specifically in their efforts to reproduce, to keep the body alive, healthy, and emotionally well adjusted. Racial domination has also allowed whites to hoard the benefits of the material labor necessary to maintain life and to secure the physical and emotional needs of the body itself as, tragically, the benefits of the forced and coerced labor of black women were among the advantages that accrued to the white body as a consequence of racial domination. Racial domination has also advantaged whites with regard to bodily integrity and reproductive health, that is, it has allowed whites to hoard the benefits not only of the labors that typically fall to women, but also of state-sponsored, positive liberty–style support and protection for women's own unique bodily needs.

Take the capability of Life. Life does not simply appear into the world. It must be reprdocued and sustained. Whites have long been advantaged relative to blacks in their efforts to reproduce – and therefore advantaged in coming into being. They have also been advantaged in their efforts to keep the body alive. And, if producing and keeping the body itself alive forms a major part of "so-called" women's work" the body politic has helped white women a great deal in their efforts while at the very least neglecting black women in their efforts to do the same. Whites have hoarded support for bringing life into being and they have done so in a racialized social context where black women where far more likely to suffer disabling reproductive intervention. Whites have therefore hoarded opportunities to produce healthy infants.

Additionally, racial domination has allowed whites to hoard opportunites to live to the end of a normal human life. Here, the American state has proved a resounding success in securing white life, particularly in securing that life from the threat of violent death.[33] Whites have hoarded the benefits of state protection for life. By contrast, even today, Lisa Miller writes, "the racialized state of American politics continues to leave African-Americans out of the promise of security from violence that many middle and even low income whites enjoy." So well has the state secured white life in particular, she writes, that "... despite the widely known gender gap in murder victims on a global scale—with men far more likely to be murdered than women—black women in the U S have been more likely to be murdered than white men for decades."[34]

The built environment is not innocent here. Among the ways in which the capability of life has been supported in whites is that they have had access to secure neighborhoods from which blacks were excluded. Blacks, who had no formal protection from the risks associated with living with others during the period of enslavement and Jim Crow (where they were at heightened risk of violent death because they were at risk of being murdered because they were black), came then to be confined in spatially isolated, resource deprived and insecure communities, with little protection from interpersonal violence.

Racial domination, including the formal denial of resources to support black bodily health under slavery and Jim Crow as well as the de facto denial under residential segregation has also allowed whites to hoard positive liberty style support for the capability of Bodily Health as well as the ability to distance themselves from things that are deleterious to health.[35] The built environment, including the placement of health enabling and health disabling resources and pathogens, factors into this. Consider here that public health scholars characterize contemporary conditions in black neighborhoods as "pathogenic," as producing "excess death" among blacks. They see "racial residential segregation" as a "fundamental cause of health disparities between blacks and whites" and see residential segregation as "the cornerstone on which black-white disparities in health status have been built in the United States."[36] Here it is important to note that Nussbaum's definition of the capability of bodily health includes reproductive health, and here, at best, black reproductive health has been neglected, at worst exploited—whether elevated or depressed—in the service of white interests.

Whites continue to hoard life- and health-enabling social contexts. Sociologists Ruth D. Peterson and Lauren J. Krivo state that even today, "[t]he stark reality of U.S. society is that whites, African Americans and Latinos live in strikingly different social worlds."[37,38] These divergent social worlds mean that even "blacks and whites of similar economic status live in dramatically different residential environments, with blacks living in areas with higher crime rates, lower quality schools, higher poverty rates, lower property values, and severe racial segregation."[39] Whites continue to hoard life and health enabling social contexts as today "whites live in the most advantaged neighborhoods, even after accounts for socioeconomic status, followed by different groups of Asian Americans and Latinos and finally black Americans."[40] It is critical that we attend to social context and not simply economic factors regarding health as scholars note that when whites make gains in income "they are able to translate this economic advantage into spatial advantage in ways that African Americans are not, by buying into communities that provide quality schools and healthy environments for their children."[41] In fact, "blacks and whites inhabit such different neighborhoods that it is not possible to compare the economic outcomes of black and white children who grow up in similarly disadvantaged neighborhoods."[42] Most blacks live under conditions white people very rarely experience, and many live under conditions virtually no whites experience. Researchers have found that half of black families lived in America's poorest neighborhoods over the last two generations, as compared to 7 percent of whites.[43]

Additionally, many scholars argue that the American variant of the welfare state, which was only belatedly extended to blacks, has been replaced by what has by turns been called a carceral state, "the

New Jim Crow" and a "prison nation," the latter a term Richie borrows from scholars who use it "to signal the situations in which a law and order social agenda has supplanted the state's willingness to provide basic material resources and opportunities for self-sufficiency for low income groups."[44] All terms are different ways of signaling a "malfare" state that has disproportionately taken the black body as its object, and disproportionately brings harm and not security to that body. Not unrelatedly contemporary theorists of American racial violence see the phenomenon as with us still but note that it has undergone a key shift from state sanctioned and neglected mob and vigilante violence to state enacted and white *and* black taxpayer financed institutionalized forms which include blacks' disproportionate experience of politic brutality, surveillance and punishment.[45]

Whites, too, have hoarded opportunities to exercise the capability of bodily integrity. First they defined the black female body as a body that invited such violations of integrity—as a body with no such integrity—by excluding black women from all formal protections for such integrity allowing whites to hoard any such positive liberty protections as might have existed. Violations of black female bodily integrity were not enshrined as a moral and legal wrong until the 1970s, in the case of Joan Little, which concerned black women's rights to defend themselves from white men's sexual advances.[46] Later still, whites excluded black women on the basis of race from secure and ordered communities that better afforded protection for such integrity. This is not to say that feminist critiques of the modern state and the minor provisions it makes to secure the bodies of women are incorrect. Rather it is to point out that first, black women were, with explicit state and legal collusion, excluded from even those minor provisions for far too long, and second, that the overall greater security afforded white bodies relative to black bodies has functioned to better protect white female bodies from physical and sexual violence. I am willing to recognize, for example, that the greater security the white female body has been afforded has been a simple byproduct of securing the white male body. Residential segregation has only helped to sustain the advantages of formal protection from physical and sexual violence white women enjoyed under Jim Crow. And it is no small thing that black women only gained legal recognition of their right to bodily integrity at the advent of the "War on Drugs"— where protecting women from sexual assault was not only not a police priority but, as Richie reports, women asked for state intervention after such assault often risked being further physically and sexually victimized by police. While the American state deserves no credit for its efforts to secure women from such phenomena as sexual assault and intimate partner violence it must answer for decades—centuries—of outright collusion in denying black women bodily integrity.

Whites have also been able to hoard opportunities to avoid having their emotional development blighted by fear and anxiety, as they have, with state support, hoarded access to safe and secure communities, that is, enabling social contexts for emotional development. They have thereby been able to hoard opportunities to develop and sustain strong emotional attachments to others and the benefits of positive liberty–style support for the family, that realm in which the physical and emotional needs of the body are met. Part of that support involved state collusion with slaveholders and later white supremacists, but also white capital and white labor, male and female, to confine black women in jobs where they helped to meet the physical and emotional needs of the white body, often at the expense of adequately meeting the same needs for their own partners and dependents.

In light of these considerations, then, corrective racial justice concerns not only establishing fair procedural rules so that whites are no longer unfairly advantaged because of intergenerational opportunity hoarding of employment and skill acquisition, resulting in an unfair distribution of income and wealth. In fact, not only must we ensure that whites are no longer unfairly advantaged in being able to live to the end of a normal life, advantaged regarding bodily health, advantaged in exercising bodily integrity and in being afforded opportunities to form strong attachments to others, but corrective justice must also endeavor to compensate blacks as well as possible in the present for the long-standing denial of these things.

Corrective racial justice requires that blacks be given greater resources for ensuring their bodily health—including enabling reproductive health services to correct for the centuries of reproductive
exploitation and neglect that blacks have endured—their bodily integrity, and their ability to form emotional attachments to others.
Justice demands, as well, direct intervention to change the pattern
of benefit of the material labor necessary to tend to the physical and
emotional needs of the black body relative to the white one, so that
whites are no longer advantaged.

Corrective racial justice must endeavor to ensure that to be born
black is not only not to be subject to intergenerational racialzied
economic disadvantage, but also not to be born into more dangerous, more pathogenic environments with fewer resources to support
health, including sexual and reproductive health, not to be born into
enviroments where one is more likely to be denied bodily integrity or
wherein heightened fear and anxiety are more likely to blight one's
abilty to form strong emotional attachments. However, in order to
correct for intergenerational white opportunity hoarding we must
ensure that black spaces are more secure, have a greater quantity and
quality of health enabling—including sexual and reproductive health,
enabling resources, have far greater resources for security bodily integrity and greater support for blacks' ability to form emotional attachments to others. This may seem straightforward but the problem
is complex, as today, to be born black is to be born less likely to have
the physical and emitonal needs of one's body met adequately *and*
to be more likely to have those needs met by someone who was less
likely to have had them adequately met and so on, across generations.
To be born black is to be more likely to be born into environments in
which one's emotional development is blighted by fear and anxiety
and to be born of and reared by someone who, too, is more likely
to be born into environments in which their emitonal devlepment
has been blighted by fear and anxiety. To be born black is to be less
likely to have access to adequate health care and to be born to someone wh was less likely to have had adequate sexual and reproductive
health care. To be born black is to have had fewer oppoertunities for

bodily integrity, to be much more likely to suffer gross violations of bodily integrity throught one's life and to have been born of someone, reared by someone, who was even more likely to have suffered such violations, again, so on across generations.

Let me state emphatically that with regards to bodily integrity, racial justice can never be realized through affording black women greater negative liberty alone, by simply promoting greater non-interference. In light of the history of gendered racial domination outlined above, black women will need far more help to realize this capability going forward, as well as the recognition that the help they need must be conceived intersectionally – where remedies sufficient to ensure bodily integrity for white women may not well serve black women. Here, it is as Mills says regarding justice behind the modified veil. We cannot assume that we are starting from a position of equality among women regarding bodily integrity. Justice demands intervening to change generations of sedimented meaning associated with black female bodies that continue to disadvantage them with regard to bodily integrity. Of course, these meaning making intervention must be led and directed by black women themselves, yet state supported. I turn to this below.

Ending white advantage regarding the ability to form strong emotional attachments to others requires not only removing overt institutional obstacles to blacks' ability to form such attachments—intervening to end disparity in abortion rates and ending the apartheid structure of foster care are two important examples—but also requires positive liberty–style institutional support for black reproduction and caretaking, including placing enabling reproductive and caretaking services in black communities. It also involves targeted efforts to make black communities more secure so that black emotional development overall is no longer disproportionately blighted by fear and anxiety.

Furthermore, in order for blacks to be be compensated for years of caretaking exploitation, black caregivers should be given greater resources to support both their own caring labor—such as enhanced parental leave—and greater access to quality child care for their dependents, so that they can work in tandem with that child care to support the physical and emotional needs of their dependents.

Providing said support will involve making significant changes in current approaches to urban planning, including transportation and housing policy. Space is currently structured by, and, as spatial feminists have argued, for men. Intimate racial justice requires transforming space to better serve the needs of women.

For example, one of the questions "gender mainstreaming" or "fair shared city" oriented urban planners ask officials to consider is whether or not female-dominated job sites are as well served by transit networks as male-dominated ones. The hub and spoke model of public transit, for example, does not well serve the needs of contemporary low wage services workers, who are disproportionately women of color with dependents and who are more likely to have multilocational job sites, often not in the center of the city.[47]

But employment accessibility is only one aspect of how planners should approach serving the needs of women. In the article, "How to Design a City for Women: A Fascinating Experiment in Gender Mainstreaming," Clare Foran writes:

> In 1999, officials in Vienna, Austria asked residents of the city's 9th district how often and why they used public transportation. "Most of the men filled out the questionnaire in less than 5 minutes, says Ursula Bauer... "But the women couldn't stop writing...Women used public transit more often and made more trips on foot than men. They were more likely to split their time between taking care of children and elderly parents. Recognizing this, city planners drafted a plan to improve pedestrian mobility and access to public transit. Additional lighting was added to make walking at night safer for women. Sidewalks were widened so pedestrians could navigate narrow streets. And a massive staircase with a ramp running through the middle was installed near a major intersection to make crossing easier for people with strollers and individuals using a walker or a wheelchair.[48]

It is possible to structure the built environment in ways that supports or in ways that undermine the work that women disproportionately do, to make streets and sidewalks safer or more dangerous, more or less accessible for women, to encourage or discourage women's use of the space. Here, city planners took care to structure the environment to better support women's uncompensated caretaking work. We need to keep projects like the one above in mind as we seek to construct a just environment for black women.

Housing policy is another area in which we must intervene to bring about intimate racial justice so that housing stock better supports and enables women's work. Black communities have longstanding housing needs that stem from residential segregation. Shelby even recognizes that changing housing policy is a part of corrective racial justice. As we address existing black housing need, we should again look to spatial feminist theory. Housing design and community planning can even be used to help reverse the flow of life supporting labor from black to white bodies—a necessary condition of intimate racial justice—and therefore justice for blacks, particularly black women, must also involve transforming the contemporary design of white communities as well.

In a classic article, "What Would a Non-Sexist City Be Like? Speculations on Housing, Urban Design, and Human Work," Dolores Hayden argues that by 1980, the idea a (white) woman's place is in the home has been an important—one of the most important—principles of urban planning for the last century.[49] She goes on to say that the policy of designing houses around the idea of a home-bound woman placed unnecessary constraints on women and that to remedy the situation it is necessary to "rehabilitate" existing housing stock and change the way houses are conceived going forward.[50] Conventional homes, she says, do not well serve the needs of working women and their families. She continues:

> Whether it is in a suburban, exurban, or inner-city neighborhood, whether it is a split-level ranch house, a modern masterpiece of

concrete and glass, or an old bring tenement, the house or apartment is almost invariably organized around the same set of
spaces: kitchen, dining room, living room, bedrooms, garage or
parking area. These spaces require someone to undertake private
cooking, cleaning, child care and usually private transportation
if adults and children are to exist within it. Because of residential zoning practices the typical dwelling will usually be physically
removed from any shared community space—no commercial or
communal day-care facilities or laundry facilities, for example,
are likely to be part of the dwelling's domain.[51]

Hayden argues against this model of housing design and holds that
justice for women requires a different model of household design:

> . . .a program to achieve economic and environmental justice for
> women requires, by definition a solution which overcomes the
> traditional divisions between the household and the market
> economy, the private dwelling and the workplace: one must
> transform the economic situation of the traditional homemaker
> whose skilled labor has been unpaid but economically and so-
> cially necessary to society; one must also transform the domi-
> nant situation of employed women.[52]

While I think that Hayden is primarily thinking of house planners'
presumptions regarding homebound white women and I strongly
disagree with her suggestion that housing policy and design disserve
women equally whether in "suburban, exurban or inner city" neighborhoods, I am intrigued by how she sees women of color and poor
women affected by housing policy designed with the homebound
middle class white woman in mind and the market based work/life
balance solutions offered to these women after the built environment fails to support their needs:

> The aids to overcome an environment without childcare, public
> transportation or food service have been "private," commercially

profitable solutions: maids and baby-sitters by the hour, fran-
chise daycare or extended television viewing; fast food service;
easier credit for purchasing an automobile, a washer or a mi-
crowave oven. Not only do these commercial solutions obscure
the failure of American housing policies, they also generate bad
conditions for other working-women. Commercial day-care and
fast food franchises are the source of low-paying nonunion jobs
without security. In this respect they resemble the use of private
household workers by bourgeois women, who may never ask how
their private maid or child-care worker arranges care for her own
children ... The logistical problems which all employed women
face are not private problems and they do not succumb to market
solutions.[53]

Hayden's proposed housing design solutions—though centered
around transforming the presumption that women do not work
and how design can facilitate women's economic participation—
are worth considering in a project to bring about justice for black
women because redesigning white and black communities in the
manner she describes would help to stem the transfer of the benefits of caring labor from blacks to whites. Hayden writes of "service houses" or "collective houses" in Copenhagen, which provided
child care and cooked food to employed women and their families.
She also writes of a housing complex designed to meet the needs of
single parents:

Children's play areas or day care centers are integrated with the
dwellings; in the Fiona House project the housing is designed
to facilitate shared baby-sitting and the day care center is open
to neighborhood residents for a fee. Thus, single parents can
find jobs as day care workers and help the neighborhood's working parents as well. What is most exciting here is that home
and work can be reunited on one site for some of the residents
and home and child care services reunited on one site for all of
them.[54]

The political community's historic collusion in violations of black female bodily integrity is a wrong that can never be set right. I think, however, public recognition of that collusion and perhaps an acknowledgment of a greater duty to protect and support black female bodily integrity in the future is a start. Justice requires devoting greater resources—discursive as well as material resources—to supporting black female bodily integrity and conceiving of all black female bodily integrity capability failures as a continuation of a founding American crime.

Justice demands, for example, that black women have a locally and black female led office devoted to ensuring black female bodily integrity, tasked with correcting the conditions—discursive and material—that threaten said integrity. The agency should be complete with victims' service centers and importantly a cultural/representational arm, the latter as recognition of the fact that the racial patriarchal culturally constructed meaning of black womanhood facilitates violence and impunity regarding said violence. Changing the racially and patriarchally constructed meaning of black womanhood must involve empowering black women to create the dominant meanings of themselves. Given the history of mistrust between black communities and police, and in the interest of trying to address the centuries of violence to which black community members have been exposed, it should include both punitive and restorative justice options as redress for assault—though it must be careful not to coerce women toward restorative options should they not desire this.

There is also important cultural/representational work that must be done and that work must be state-supported but black female led, given the state's role in constructing and supporting a problematic meanings of black womanhood that continues to expose black women to disproportionate violence in their already insecure communities. Key in ensuring black female bodily integrity is changing the meaning of black womanhood—that is representational work—so that, for example, black women are no longer blamed for the assaults they experience. I would not recommend censorship but instead argue that justice requires state support for black women's artistic work—films, media, commercials and the like—so that the larger political community and public sphere are forced to contend with black women's definition of themselves.

Part of supporting black women's bodily integrity involves protecting them from their disproportionate exposure to violence. Again, the built environment is implicated in this. Hayden writes of how housing patterns facilitate intimate partner violence and she speculates that there is a relationship between household isolation, women's uncompensated labor and battering. She says, "The woman who does leave the isolated single family house or apartment finds very few real housing alternatives available to her. The typical divorced or battered woman is currently seeking housing, employment and childcare simultaneously—she finds that matching her complex family requirements with the various available offerings by landlords, employers and social services is impossible."[55] She goes on to say, "One environment that unites housing, services and jobs could resolve many of the difficulties."[56] Hayden raises excellent points. We know from Richie's work, however, that black women in underresourced communities are not well served by the conservative model of gender-based violence prevention. These models have become entrenched, she says, even as the violence black women face— community and police violence as well as intimate partner violence—looks very different from the forms of violence white women face, with some of it—at the intersection of gender based violence and racialized housing shortages—resembling human trafficking. Therefore, we must ensure that all spatial design devoted to ending the problem of gender based violence in black communities be conceived intersectionally.

Any corrective racial justice project must explicitly address black women's intergenerational experience of injustice in the intimate sphere. Addressing these longstanding and compounding injustices requires, at a minimum, that greater resources be devoted to protecting black female bodily integrity so that they are no longer more likely to have said bodily integrity violated than white women, that greater resources be devoted to ensuring black bodily health, including black female reproductive health, so that their reproductive health outcomes are at the very least on par with white women, and that greater resources be devoted to enabling blacks' abilities to form emotional attachments to others such that black partners and caretakers are able to spend as much time nurturing those attachments—not working and commuting—and that they may do so under the same conditions and relative safety as whites. As well, a just outcome requires that said greater resources be ceded to the direction and control of local women in black communities who are committed to an intersectional approach to ensuring these intimate capabilities for generations to come.

NOTES

Preface

1. Blacks were considered the "syphilitic race" in the 1930s and therefore destined to die out.
2. David Zucchino, "Sterilized by North Carolina, She Felt Raped Once More," *Los Angeles Times*, January 25, 2012. "They butchered me like a hog," she adds.
3. "The Rebecca Project works diligently to reform intersecting health, child welfare, and criminal justice policies impacting vulnerable families. Among our primary advocacy goals are expanding comprehensive family treatment services, improving conditions of confinement for incarcerated women and girls, promoting alternative sentencing for women and girls, challenging the unacceptable levels of gendered violence, and urging for policies of health and healing for families at the margins."

   We measure the outcomes to our stated goals in the following ways: (a) appropriation gains to expand family-based treatment, (b) number of bills that include sentencing alternatives to maternal incarceration, (c) improved conditions of maternal incarceration and parent-child relationship during a mother's sentence, and (d) elevated visibility on violence against vulnerable women and girls." The Rebecca Project, "Our Work: US Policy and Goals," http://www.rebeccaprojectjustice.org/index. php?option=com_content&task=blogcategory&id=20&Itemid=52

167

4. Obama himself was forced to acknowledge issues affecting young black women by Kimberlé Crenshaw and other black feminist activists who criticized the explicit masculine focus of his "My Brother's Keeper" program.
5. Beth Richie, *Arrested Justice: Black Women, Violence, and America's Prison Nation* (New York: New York University Press, 2012), 9–10.

Chapter 1

1. bell hooks, *Feminist Theory from Margin to Center* (Boston: South End Press, 1984), 134.
2. Audre Lorde, "Age, Race, Class and Sex: Women Redefining Difference," in *Words of Fire: An Anthology of African-American Feminist Thought*, ed. Beverly Guy-Sheftall (New York: The New Press, 1995), 288.
3. Dorothy Roberts, *Killing the Black Body: Race, Reproduction and the Meaning of Liberty* (New York: Vintage, 1997), 93.
4. "In the South, rendering black women infertile without their knowledge during other surgery was so common that the procedure was called a 'Mississippi Appendectomy.'" Harriet A. Washington, *Medical Apartheid: The Dark History of Medical Experimentation on Black Americans from Colonial Times to the Present* (New York: Anchor Press, 2008), 204.
5. For an account of the history of racialized reproductive control see Rickie Solinger, *Pregnancy and Power: A Short History of Reproductive Politics in America* (New York: New York University Press, 2007). See also Rickie Solinger, *Wake Up Little Susie: Single Pregnancy and Race before Roe* (New York: Routledge, 1994).
6. "In 1964, the SNCC issued a pamphlet called 'Genocide in Mississippi' that contained critical information about a punitive sterilization bill in Mississippi, making it a felony to give birth to a second or subsequent illegitimate child. Those convicted would be sterilized. . . . [Fannie Lou] Hamer testified about her forced sterilization at the 1964 Democratic convention in Atlantic city. . . . In a speech before the Women's International League for Peace and Freedom, Hamer reported that 60 percent of all women who passed through Sunflower City Hospital in her hometown in Mississippi were sterilized, many without their knowledge." Jennifer Nelson, *Women of Color and the Reproductive Rights Movement* (New York: New York University Press, 2003), 67, 68.
7. "When [the Southern Poverty Law Center] filed a class-action lawsuit to end the use of federal funds for involuntary sterilization, its lawyers discovered that 100,000 to 150,000 women had been sterilized using federal funds and that half of these women were black. Today, one

third of all adult Mississippi women and 57 percent of all Mississippi women sixty-five and older say they have undergone an hysterectomy." Harriet A. Washington, *Medical Apartheid: The Dark History of Medical Experimentation on Black Americans from Colonial Times to the Present* (New York: Doubleday, 2006), 204.

8. Nelson, *Women of Color and the Reproductive Rights Movement*.
9. Classical phase 1954–1965, the Montgomery Boycott to the 1965 Voting Rights Act. Bayard Rustin, "From Protest to Politics: The Future of the Civil Rights Movement," *Commentary* 39, no. 2, February 1, 1965.
10. "The disjuncture between movement ideals and practices, along with her growing awareness of sterilization abuse among women of color, prompted Beal, a former NAACP youth leader and member of SNCC's International Affairs Commission, to present a paper at a 1968 SNCC personnel meeting in New York. As part of this paper, Beal recommended that SNCC form a black women's caucus to explore the impact of sexism on the organizations constituency in addition to racism.... Similar to Beal's attention to sterilization abuse as a reproductive rights issue for black women, Sloan and members of the [National Black Feminist Organization] noted the sexist rhetoric that the recent Supreme Court decision in *Roe v. Wade* had sparked. Noting black nationalist denouncements of the pro-abortion decision as genocide and the women's movement's singular focus on abortion as the only reproductive rights issue prompted black women in New York to consider feminism as a viable political option." Kimberly Springer, *Living for the Revolution: Black Feminist Organizations, 1968–1980* (Durham, NC: Duke University Press, 2005), 47, 51.
11. Jael Miriam Silliman, Marlene Gerber Fried, Loretta Ross, and Elana R. Gutierrez, *Undivided Rights: Women of Color Organize for Reproductive Justice* (Cambridge, MA: South End Press, 2004), 49. Johanna Schoen states, "Policy makers and health and welfare professionals have frequently assumed that poor single mothers—particularly if they were African American, Hispanic or Native American—lacked the ability to function properly as mothers and that they should be discouraged from further childbearing." Johanna Schoen, *Choice and Coercion: Birth Control, Sterilization, and Abortion in Public Health and Welfare* (Chapel Hill: The University of North Carolina Press, 2005), 5.
12. Nelson, *Women of Color and the Reproductive Rights Movement*; Schoen, *Choice and Coercion*.
13. The women also discussed their access to decent health care, adoption, and the abuse of native children in foster care. Silliman et al., *Undivided Rights*, 110.
14. Silliman et al., *Undivided Rights*, 111.

15. Silliman et al., *Undivided Rights*, 226–227.
16. Silliman et al., *Undivided Rights*, 225.
17. Frances Beal, "Double Jeopardy: To Be Black and Female," in *Words of Fire: An Anthology of African-American Feminist Thought; Beverly Guy-Sheftall* (New York: The New Press, 2013), 151–152.
18. Silliman et al., *Undivided Rights*, 49.
19. Nelson, *Women of Color and the Reproductive Rights Movement*, 80–81.
20. Nelson, *Women of Color and the Reproductive Rights Movement*, 3–4, 15.
21. Nelson, *Women of Color and the Reproductive Rights Movement*, 81.
22. Roberts, *Killing the Black Body*; Nelson, *Women of Color and the Reproductive Rights Movement*; Silliman et al., *Undivided Rights*; Springer, *Living for the Revolution*; Solinger, *Wake Up Little Susie*; Solinger, *Pregnancy and Power*.
23. Toni Morrison, *Beloved*, (New York: Knopf Doubleday Publishing Group, 2007), xvi.
24. In *Killing the Black Body* Roberts points out that women of color, and black women specifically, are routinely singled out for longer-lasting and more permanent forms of birth control. Anna Marie Smith and Rickie Solinger agree with Roberts' assessment. Smith notes, "Poor mothers, and poor women of color in particular, have been consistently singled out for the most severe types of population management tactics." Solinger states, "Government [fertility management] efforts have most pointedly targeted women of color." Roberts, *Killing the Black Body*, 108–109; Anna Marie Smith, *Welfare Reform and Sexual Regulation* (New York: Cambridge University Press, 2007), 14; Solinger, *Pregnancy and Power*, 132. "Many white, male researchers and health professionals assumed that poor and minority women were unable or unmotivated to use contraceptives properly and encouraged the development and testing of cheaper contraceptives and contraceptives that were outside the control of female patients." Schoen, *Choice and Coercion*, 5.
25. "In summary, the foster care system in the nation's cities acts as an apartheid institution. . . . Today, *42 percent of all children in foster care nationwide are Black,* even though Black children constitute only 17 percent of the nation's youth." Dorothy Roberts, *Shattered Bonds: The Color of Child Welfare* (New York: Basic Books, 2003), 7–8, 10.
26. Richard Iton, *In Search of the Black Fantastic: Politics and Popular Culture in the post–Civil Rights Era* (New York: Oxford University Press, 2008).
27. Ula Y. Taylor, "Black Feminisms and Human Agency," in *No Permanent Waves: Recasting Histories of U.S. Feminism*, ed. Nancy A. Hewitt (New Brunswick, NJ: Rutgers University Press, 2010).
28. Taylor, "Black Feminisms," 62.

29. Bayard Rustin coined the term "classical phase" to name the period between the Supreme Court's 1954 ruling on school desegregation and the 1964 Civil Rights Act. Rustin, "From Protest to Politics."
30. Taylor, "Black Feminisms," 61.
31. Iris Marion Young, *Justice and the Politics of Difference* (Princeton, NJ: Princeton University Press, 2011), 40.
32. The Combahee River Collective, "A Black Feminist Statement," in *Words of Fire: An Anthology of African-American Feminist Thought*, ed. Beverly Guy-Sheftall (New York: New Press, 1995), 232.
33. Jacqueline Jones, *Labor of Love, Labor of Sorrow: Black Women, Work, and the Family from Slavery to the Present* (New York: Basic Books, 1985), 1–2.
34. Phyllis M. Palmer, *Domesticity and Dirt: Housewives and Domestic Servants in the United States, 1920–1945* (Philadelphia: Temple University Press, 1989), 70.
35. See Tera W. Hunter, *To 'joy My Freedom: Southern Black Women's Lives and Labors after the Civil War* (Cambridge, Mass.: Harvard University Press, 1997), 114–120.
36. White workers employed "hate strikes" in order to block black promotions from menial to semiskilled and skilled labor at a factory. Thus, the workers attacked blacks, not capitalists.
37. Taylor, "Black Feminisms," 62.
38. Catherine A. MacKinnon and Reva B. Siegel, eds., *Directions in Sexual Harassment Law* (New Haven, CT: Yale University Press, 2004).
39. Deborah Gray White, *A'r'n't I a Woman? Female Slaves in the Plantation South* (New York: Norton, 1985).
40. John Hope Franklin and Loren Schweninger, *Runaway Slaves: Rebels on the Plantation* (New York: Oxford University Press, 1999).
41. Ida B. Wells-Barnett, *On Lynchings* (Amherst, NY: Humanity Books, 2002).
42. Darlene Clark Hine, "Rape and the Inner Lives of Black Women in the Middle West: Preliminary Thoughts on the Culture of Dissemblance," in *Words of Fire: An Anthology of African-American Feminist Thought*, ed. Beverly Guy-Sheftall (New York: New Press, 1995), 386.
43. Evelyn Brooks Higginbotham, *Righteous Discontent: The Women's Movement in the Black Baptist Church, 1880–1920* (Cambridge: Harvard University Press, 1993).
44. Taylor, "Black Feminisms," 65.
45. Evelyn Nakano Glenn, "From Servitude to Service Work: Historical Continuities in the Racial Division of Paid Reproductive Labor," *Signs: Journal of Women in Culture and Society* 18, no. 1 (1992): 1–43. See also Elsa Barkley Brown, "What Has Happened Here: The Politics of Difference in Women's History and Feminist Politics," in *The Second Wave: A Reader*

in Feminist Theory, ed. Linda J. Nicholson (New York: Routledge, 1997), 272–285.
46. Hunter, *To 'joy My Freedom*, 111.
47. bell hooks, "Black Women: Shaping Feminist Theory," in *Words of Fire: An Anthology of African-American Feminist Thought*, ed. Beverly Guy-Sheftall (New York: New Press, 1995), 270.
48. hooks, "Black Women," 270.
49. This is not to say that black women did not work to improve workplace relations.
50. hooks, *Feminist Theory from Margin to Center*, 133.
51. Premilla Nadasen, *Welfare Warriors: The Welfare Rights Movement in the United States* (New York: Routledge, 2004), xviii–xix.
52. It should be noted that hooks is responding to a somewhat mythical Friedan. Daniel Horowitz states that Friedan, in fact, grew up in a radical Jewish household and created the bored-housewife myth to distance feminism from left-wing radicalism; Horowitz suggests that she herself may have come to believe the myth she created. She continued to organize around racial and class equality after her marriage. Daniel Horowitz, *Betty Friedan and the Making of the Feminine Mystique: The American Left, the Cold War, and Modern Feminism* (Amherst: University of Massachusetts Press, 1998).
53. Beal spoke the truth. Evelyn Nakano Glenn notes: "In the domestic sphere, instead of questioning the inequitable gender division of labor, [middle-class women] sought to slough off the more burdensome tasks onto more oppressed groups of women. . . . Domestics were employed to clean house, launder and iron clothes, scrub floors, and care for infants and children. They relieved their mistresses of the heavier and dirtier domestic chores. White middle-class women were thereby freed for supervisory tasks and for cultural, leisure, and volunteer activity or, more rarely during this period, for a career." Evelyn Nakano Glenn, "From Servitude to Service Work," 7.
54. Beal, "Double Jeopardy," 111.
55. Brown, "What Has Happened Here," 272–285.
56. Susan Bordo, "Unbearable Weight: Feminism, Western Culture, and the Body," 18.
57. Nelson, *Women of Color and the Reproductive Rights Movement*, 5–6.
58. Nelson, *Women of Color and the Reproductive Rights Movement*, 15.
59. Angela Y. Davis, *Women, Race, and Class* (New York: Vintage Books, 1983), 204.
60. Audre Lorde, *Sister Outsider: Essays and Speeches* (Berkeley, CA: Crossing Press, 2007), 74.
61. Lorde, "Age, Race, Class and Sex," 119.

62. Lorde, "Age, Race, Class and Sex," 119.
63. Lorde, "Age, Race, Class and Sex," 119.
64. Lorde, "Age, Race, Class and Sex," 119.
65. "One of the chief contributions of feminist thought to political theory in the western tradition is to have questioned the line dividing the public and the private. Feminists have argued that the 'privacy' of the private sphere, which has always included the relations of the male head of household to his spouse and children, has been an opaque glass rendering women and their traditional spheres of activity invisible and inaudible. Two centuries after the American and the French revolutions, the entry of women into the public sphere is far from complete, the gender division of labor in the family is still not the object of moral and political reflection, and women and their concerns are still invisible in contemporary theories of justice and community" (Seyla Benhabib, *Situating the Self: Gender, Community and Postmodernism in Contemporary Ethics* (New York: Routledge, 1992), 12–13). The result, Benhabib argues, is that "[a]n entire domain of human activity, namely, nurture, reproduction, love and care, which becomes the women's lot in the course of the development of the modern, bourgeois society, is excluded from moral and political consideration and relegated to the realm of 'nature' (155)." Kathie Sarachild outlined the disagreements within the New Left which spawned the feminist insight "the personal is political" in "Consciousness Raising: A Radical Weapon": "The methods and assumptions behind consciousness-raising essentially grew out of both the scientific and radical political traditions, but when we applied them to women's situation a whole set of otherwise 'scientific' and 'radical' people—especially men—just couldn't see this. Whole areas of women's lives were declared off limits to discussion. Topics we were talking about in our groups they dismissed as 'petty' or 'not political.' Often these were the key areas in terms of how women are oppressed as a particular group—like housework, childcare, and sex." Kathie Sarachild, "Consciousness-Raising: A Radical Weapon," in *Feminist Revolution*, ed. Kathie Sarachild (New York: Random House, 1978), 145.
66. Benhabib, *Situating the Self*, 12–13.
67. Benhabib, *Situating the Self*, 13.
68. Benhabib, *Situating the Self*, 107–108.
69. Susan Moller Okin, *Justice, Gender and the Family* (New York: Basic Books, 1991); Carole Pateman, *The Sexual Contract* (Stanford, CA: Stanford University Press, 1988).
70. Nancy Fraser and Axel Honneth, *Redistribution or Recognition? A Political-Philosophical Exchange* (New York: Verso, 2003).
71. Young, *Justice and the Politics of Difference*, 16.

72. Young, *Justice and the Politics of Difference*, 19.
73. Young, *Justice and the Politics of Difference*, 16.
74. Robert Gooding-Williams, *In the Shadow of Du Bois: Afro-Modern Political Thought in America* (Cambridge, MA: Harvard University Press, 2009).
75. Gooding-Williams, 4.
76. Gooding-Williams, 10.
77. In fact, so thoroughly entwined were Plato's hatred of the body and his misogyny that he was often able to make remarkably nonsexist remarks regarding women and their potential contributions to society when he was not thinking about the body. Conversely, however, when he did think of the body, his thoughts returned almost immediately to women and those same thoughts immediately veered towards the misogynistic. Elizabeth V. Spelman "Woman as Body: Ancient and Contemporary Views," *Feminist Studies* 8 (Spring 1982): 109–131, 119.
78. Moira Gatens, *Imaginary Bodies: Ethics, Power and Corporeality* (New York: Routledge, 1996).
79. Pateman, *The Sexual Contract*.
80. Ruth Perry, "Mary Astell and the Feminist Critique of Possessive Individualism," *Eighteenth-Century Studies* 23, no. 4 (1990): 444–457.
81. Roberts, *Killing the Black Body*, 23.
82. Susan L. Thomas notes that "[b]y mid-1995, 70 bills in 35 states had been proposed on Norplant's availability, most offered financial inducements to women on welfare to use Norplant or that make Norplant use a condition of welfare receipt." Susan L. Thomas, "Race, Gender and Welfare Reform: The Antinatalist Response," *Journal of Black Studies* 4 (1998): 434.
83. "The state regulates and criminalizes reproduction for many poor women through mandatory or discriminatory promotion of long-acting contraceptives and sterilization, and by charging pregnant women on drugs with negligence or child abuse." Jael Miriam Silliman, Anannya Bhattacharjee, and Angela Y. Davis, *Policing the National Body: Sex, Race and Criminalization* (Cambridge, MA: South End Press, 2002), xi. Rickie Solinger, like Roberts, links reproductive control in slavery to contemporary fertility regulation, noting "how first slave owners and then social critics, politicians and people who work in social service agencies claimed authority and power over the lives of poor, relatively powerless, fertile women through their reproductive capacity." Solinger, *Pregnancy and Power*, 6.

Chapter 2

1. Toni Morrison, *Beloved*, Foreword (New York: Vintage, 2004), xvi.
2. Jennifer L. Morgan, *Laboring Women: Reproduction and Gender in New World Slavery* (Philadelphia: University of Pennsylvania Press, 2004), 131–132.

3. Gayl Jones, *Corregidora* (Boston: Beacon Press, 1987).
4. Mark Reinhardt, "Who Speaks for Margaret Garner? Slavery, Silence, and the Politics of Ventriloquism," *Critical Inquiry* 29, no. 1 (2002): 81–119, 93. Reinhardt goes on to say, "This choice of death before slavery revealed not only the horrors of the peculiar institution but the true character of those who were unjustly subjected. Garner's heroism and love of freedom were staples of commentary by not only active abolitionists but also more politically respectable critics of the slave south. In referring to the 'excitement' and 'thrills' provided by the case, they commonly invoked the intensity of her resistance to slavery. Abolitionists, of course, pushed the point especially far."
5. Paul Gilroy, *The Black Atlantic: Modernity and Double Consciousness* (Cambridge, MA: Harvard University Press, 2005), 64.
6. Frances E.W. Harper, "The Slave Mother: A Tale of Ohio," in *Complete Poems of Frances E.W. Harper*, ed. Maryemma Graham (New York: Oxford University Press, 1988), 28–30.
7. Frances E.W. Harper, *Iola Leroy, or Shadows Uplifted* (Penguin, 2010).
8. Ashraf H.A. Rushdy, "Daughters Signifyin(g) History: The Example of Toni Morrison's *Beloved*," in *Toni Morrison's* Beloved: *A Casebook*, ed. William L. Andrews and Nellie Y. McKay, 37–66, 43–44.
9. Angela Y. Davis, "Reflections on the Black Woman's Role in the Community of Slaves," *The Massachusetts Review* 13, nos. 1/2 (1972): 81–100.
10. "By 1981, Angela Y. Davis would echo [Herbert Aptheker] in arguing that the Margaret Garner case demonstrated not only the willingness of slave women to organize insurrections but also the unique desperation of the slave mother," Rushdy writes in "Daughters Signifyin(g) History," 44. bell hooks does not mention Garner specifically, but does thematize the issue of mass sexual assault (problematically labeled as "prostitution" by abolitionists), the prevalence of sexual assault in women's reflections on slavery, the scant knowledge enslaved women possessed with regard to their bodies and reproduction, and the fact that women and men often performed the same productive labor tasks in "Sexism and the Black Female Slave Experience." She also references Davis. bell hooks, "Sexism and the Black Female Slave Experience," in *Ain't I a Woman: Black Women and Feminism* (Boston: South End Press, 1981), 15–49.
11. Gilroy, *The Black Atlantic*, 66.
12. Richard Yarborough, "Race, Violence and Manhood: The Masculine Ideal in Frederick Douglass's 'The Heroic Slave,'" in *Frederick Douglass: New Literary and Historical Essays*. ed. Eric J. Sundquist. (New York: Cambridge Univ. Press, 1990), 166–188. Douglass is not alone in this. Valerie Smith notes that "the narratives of male slaves often link the escape to freedom to the act of physically subduing the master." Valerie Smith,

Self-Discovery and Authority in Afro-American Narrative (Cambridge, MA: Harvard University Press, 1987), 33.

13. Frederick Douglass, *Narrative of the Life of Frederick Douglass, an American Slave, Written by Himself* (New York: Oxford University Press, 1999). I see the attention to violence as an important conceptual innovation in black political thought. I address the issue of violence in black–white relations with Du Bois in the next chapter. Whether or not these relationships can be repaired are central questions within black nationalist and self-defense discourse (or in the case of the African Blood Brotherhood—a radical black secret society established by Cyril Briggs in New York City in 1919—both).

14. Claudia Tate, *Domestic Allegories of Political Desire: The Black Heroine's Text at the Turn of the Century* (New York: Oxford University Press, 1996), 81. I would add confrontation against identifiable agents of racial subordination.

15. Thomas Hobbes, *Leviathan,* (New York: Oxford University Press, 1994), Isaiah Berlin, "Two Concepts of Liberty," in *Four Essays on Liberty* (London: Oxford University Press, 2002).

16. Morgan, *Laboring Women.*

17. Barbara Bush-Slimani, "Hard Labour: Women, Childbirth and Resistance in British Caribbean Slave Societies," *History Workshop Journal* 36 (1993): 84.

18. Deborah Gray White, *A'r'n't I a Woman? Female Slaves in the Plantation South* (New York: Norton, 1985), 69. See also Morgan, *Laboring Women,* 104–105.

19. Barbara Bush, *Slave Women in Caribbean Society, 1650–1838* (Kingston: Heinemann Publishers, 1990). The field has expanded in the last twenty-five years to include Stephanie Camp's *Closer to Freedom: Enslaved Women and Everyday Resistance in the Plantation South* (Chapel Hill: University of North Carolina Press, 2004). There are also documentary accounts, including Patricia Morton, ed., *Discovering the Women in Slavery: Emancipating Perspectives on the American Past* (Athens: University of Georgia Press, 1996), and anthologies such as David Barry Gaspar and Darlene Clark Hines's *More Than Chattel: Black Women and Slavery in the Americas* (Bloomington: Indiana University Press, 1996). When Deborah Gray White published *A'r'n't I A Woman* the Library of Congress had to create a new designation for Women and Slavery, as none existed before. Deborah Gray White, *Telling Histories: Black Women Historians in the Ivory Tower* (Chapel Hill: University of North Carolina Press, 2008).

20. Harriet Jacobs, *Incidents in the Life of a Slave Girl—Written by Herself,* ed. Jean Fagan Yellin (Cambridge, MA: Harvard University Press, 1987), 79.

21. Angela Y. Davis, *Women, Race, and Class* (New York: Vintage Books, 1983), 6.
22. Dorothy Roberts, *Killing the Black Body: Race, Reproduction and the Meaning of Liberty* (New York: Vintage, 1997), 29.
23. Morgan, *Laboring Women*, 100.
24. Morgan, *Laboring Women*, 3.
25. Harriet A. Washington, *Medical Apartheid: The Dark History of Medical Experimentation on Black Americans from Colonial Times to the Present* (New York: Anchor Press, 2008), 2.
26. Washington, *Medical Apartheid*, 3.
27. Washington, *Medical Apartheid*, 7.
28. Washington, *Medical Apartheid*, 7–8.
29. Washington, *Medical Apartheid*, 8.
30. Jenny Franchot, "The Punishment of Esther: Frederick Douglass and the Construction of the Feminine," in *Frederick Douglass: New Literary and Historical Essays*. ed. Eric J. Sundquist (New York: Cambridge University Press, 1990), 141–165, 149.
31. Jacobs, *Incidents*.
32. Hazel V. Carby, *Reconstructing Womanhood: The Emergence of the Afro-American Woman Novelist* (New York: Oxford University Press, 1987), 47.
33. Washington, *Medical Apartheid*, 3.
34. Gilroy, The Black Atlantic, 66.
35. Gilroy, The Black Atlantic, 66.
36. Saidiya Hartmann, *Scenes of Subjection: Terror, Slavery and Self-Making in Nineteenth Century America* (New York: Oxford University Press, 1997), 120.
37. Smith, *Self-Discovery*, 9–10.
38. Wilson Jeremiah Moses, *Creative Conflict in African American Thought: Frederick Douglass, Alexander Crummell, Booker T. Washington, W.E.B. Du Bois, and Marcus Garvey* (New York: Cambridge University Press, 2004), 23.
39. Moses, *Creative Conflict*, 46.
40. Moses, *Creative Conflict*, 46, 48.
41. Moses, *Creative Conflict*, 23–24, 56.
42. Moses, *Creative Conflict*, 33.
43. In his note 7 Moses specifies the feminist critics. "Mary Helen Washington, acknowledging the influences of Valerie Smith and Hazel Carby, makes valid observations on the limitations of Douglass' masculinist paradigms in *Invented Lives: Narratives of Black Women* (Garden City, NY: Doubleday, 1987), 8."

44. Like the prototypical *Bildungsroman*, however, the plot does not adequately accommodate differences in male and female development. Smith, *Self-Discovery*, 27, 33.
45. Smith, *Self-Discovery*, 34.
46. Smith, *Self-Discovery*, 23.
47. Douglass, *Narrative*, 55–56.
48. Douglass, *Narrative*, 56.
49. Douglass, *Narrative*, 25.
50. Smith, *Self-Discovery*, 25.
51. Tate, *Domestic Allegories*, 29.
52. "John Blassingame, in *The Slave Community*, concluded that Jacobs's narrative is inauthentic because it does not conform to the guidelines of representativeness. Blassingame questioned the narrative's orderly framework and the use of providential encounters and continued: 'the story is too melodramatic: miscegenation and cruelty, outraged virtue, unrequited love, and planter licentiousness appear on practically every page.' . . . In comparing slave narratives to each other, historians and literary critics have relied on a set of unquestioned assumptions that interrelate the quest for freedom and literacy with the establishment of manhood in the gaining of the published, and therefore public, voice. . . . The criteria for judgment that Blassingame advances here leave no room for a consideration of the specificity and uniqueness of the black female experience." Carby, *Reconstructing Womanhood*, 45–46.
53. Jacobs, *Incidents*, 26.
54. Jacobs, *Incidents*, 83.
55. Jacobs, *Incidents*, 26–27.
56. Jacobs, *Incidents*, 27.
57. Mary Prince, for example, speaks of "the black morning" when her mother told her mistress, "I am going to carry my little chickens to market, take your last look of them; may be you will see them no more." Her mother lined them up, their backs against the wall, and "When the sale was over, my mother hugged and kissed us and mourned over us, begging of us to keep up a good heart and do our duty to our new masters. It was a sad party, one went one way, one another; and our poor mammy went home with nothing." Mary Prince, *The Historo of Mary Prince: A West Indian Slave Narrative* (North Chelmsford, MA: Courier Corporation, 2004), 6, 8.
58. Jacobs, *Incidents*, 82.
59. Jacobs, *Incidents*, 85.
60. Jacobs, *Incidents*, 84–85.

61. Jacobs, *Incidents*, 136–137. She goes on to say, "My friends feared I should become a cripple for life and I was so weary of my long imprisonment that had it not been for the hope of serving my children I should have been thankful to die; but for their sake I was willing to bear on." Jacobs, *Incidents*, 192.
62. Gray White, *A'r'n't I a Woman?*, 71.
63. Deborah Gray White, "Let My People Go: 1804–1860," in *To Make Our World Anew: A History of African Americans*, ed. Robert D.G. Kelley and Earl Lewis (New York: Oxford University Press, 2000), 169–226,195.
64. Jacobs, *Incidents*, 302.
65. "Steven Weisenburger has made an extended circumstantial case that Archibald Gaines probably fathered one or more of Margaret's children.... First, Sam, Mary and Cilla, all notably lighter than their brother Tom, were the three children born after Archibald bought Margaret from his brother, during a period in which he would have been the only white male at Maplewood." Mark Reinhardt, *Who Speaks for Margaret Garner?: The True Story That Inspired Toni Morrison's Beloved* (Minneapolis: University of Minnesota Press, 2010), 14.
66. "For antebellum census-takers were always precise about parsing a master's slave property as either 'black' or 'mulatto,' depending on whether the person had one-eighth or more of white ancestry, and this is how we know that while Duke and Priscilla (Margaret's mother) were always listed in census records as 'black,' Margaret was characterized as 'mulatto.' Who then was her father? We know from his own records that, in 1833, John Gaines was the only white male residing at Maplewood. Moreover, there is nothing in the record about Priscilla being 'hired out,' elsewhere.... That John Gaines was Margaret's father is therefore a reasonable suspicion." Steven Weisenburger, "A Historical Margaret Garner," excerpted from *Modern Medea: A Family Story of Slavery and Child Murder from the Old South* (New York: Hill and Wang, 1998).
67. Spillers, "Mama's Baby, Papa's Maybe: An American Grammar Book," *Diacritics* 17, o. 2 (1987): 64–81, 80.
68. Spillers, "Mama's Baby, Papa's Maybe," 80.
69. Darlene Clark Hine, "Rape and the Inner Lives of Black Women in the Middle West: Preliminary Thoughts on the Culture of Dissemblance," in *Words of Fire: An Anthology of African-American Feminist Thought*, ed. Beverly Guy-Sheftall (New York: New Press, 1995), 380–388, 384.
70. Spillers, "Mama's Baby, Papa's Maybe," 80.
71. Spillers, "Mama's Baby, Papa's Maybe," 79–80.

72. Spillers, "Mama's Baby, Papa's Maybe," 80. "Sapphire" refers to one of the dominant stereotypical representations of black women, which include the fiery castrating Sapphire who battles male characters; the mammy, who is matronly, beyond reproductive age, and cares more for white children than her own (and is thus content to rear without the power to name, to care without full decision-making power in the process); the sexually promiscuous jezebel; and the tragic mulatta, caught between two worlds, black and white. Among the four, "in the stereotype of Sapphire, African American women are portrayed as evil, bitchy, stubborn and hateful. In other words, Sapphire is everything that Mammy is not." Marilyn Yarbrough with Crystal Bennett, "Cassandra and the 'Sistahs': The Peculiar Treatment of African American Women in the Myth of Women as Liars," *Journal of Gender, Race and Justice* 3-2 (1999–2000): 625–658, 638. While the other three images function independently, Sapphire is a relational character, depicted in relationship to the black man whom she tirelessly berates. "When the sapphire image is portrayed it is the African American male who represents the point of contention, in an ongoing verbal dual between Sapphire and the African American male." K. Sue Jewell, *From Mammy to Miss America and Beyond: Cultural Images and the Shaping of U.S. Social Policy* (New York: Routledge, 2002), 45. Within the dominant culture, it is used to highlight black male moral corruption. Jewell states that most often men, both African American and others, do not take Sapphire seriously, "and refer to her constant bossiness, dismissing her by saying, 'You're always running your mouth.'" Jewell, *From Mammy to Miss America*, 45. Political theorists must not do this.
73. Nancy Hirschmann, *The Subject of Liberty: Toward a Feminist Theory of Freedom* (Princeton, NJ: Princeton University Press, 2003).
74. Gilroy, *The Black Atlantic*, 66.
75. Isaiah Berlin, "Two Concepts of Liberty," in *Four Essays on Liberty* (Oxford: Oxford University Press, 1969), 166–217, 169.
76. Hirschmann, *The Subject of Liberty*, 137.
77. Hirschmann, *The Subject of Liberty*, 23.
78. Hirschmann, *The Subject of Liberty*, 122.
79. Richie, *Arrested Justice: Black Women, Violence, and America's Prison Nation* (New York: New York University Press, 2012), 26.
80. Richie, *Arrested Justice*, 29.
81. Lisa L. Miller, "Racialized State Failure and the Violent Death of Michael Brown," *Theory & Event* 17, no. 3 (2014), Beth Richie 2012. Richie: 17.
82. Kimberle Williams Crenshaw, "Mapping the Margins: Intersectionality, Identity Politics, and Violence Against Women of Color," *Stanford Law Review* 43, no. 6 (1991): 1241–1299, 1268–1269.

Chapter 3

1. Rayford Logan, *The Negro in American Life and Thought: The Nadir, 1877–1901* (New York: Dial Press, 1954).
2. Jessie P. Guzman and W. Hardin Hughes, "Lynching-Crime," in *Negro Year Book: A Review of Events Affecting Negro Life, 1944–1946, 1947*, ed. Jessie P. Guzman (Tuskegee, AL: Tuskegee Institute, 1947), 302–311. "Between 1886–1900, more than 2,500 lynchings of blacks occurred as whites resorted to violence to enforce black subordination.... Between 1900 and 1931, 566 lynchings were reported in the South, in which 97 percent of the victims were black. Throughout the Jim Crow era, hundreds of blacks were maimed, jailed, intimidated, or otherwise terrorized for racial dissent—or even just for being black." Angela M. Hornsby, "Gender and Class in Post-Emancipation Black Communities," in *A Companion to African American History*, ed. Alton Hornsby Jr. (New York: Blackwell Publishing, 2004) 381–394, 381.
3. I distinguish between early-twentieth-century race riots and the black-led uprisings of the 1960s.
4. Joy James, *Shadowboxing: Representations of Black Feminist Politics* (New York: Palgrave Macmillan, 2002), 48; Ida B. Wells, *On Lynchings: Southern Horrors, A Red Record, Mob Rule in New Orleans* (Amherst, NY: Humanity Books, 2002).
5. Evelyn Brooks Higginbotham, *Righteous Discontent: The Women's Movement in the Black Baptist Church, 1880–1920* (Cambridge, MA: Harvard University Press, 1993), 101.
6. Higginbotham, *Righteous Discontent*, 101.
7. Higginbotham, 101. Joanna P. Moore, founder of the "Training School for Wives and Mothers," gives a first-hand account of the events. Joanna P. Moore, *"In Christ's Stead": Autobiographical Sketches* (New York: Women's Baptist Home Mission Society, 1902), 159–163.
8. Higginbotham, *Righteous Discontent*, 101.
9. Higginbotham, *Righteous Discontent*, 101.
10. Freedmen often quit their "home places" to join wives and children on lands owned by the former owners of their families, thereby making no small contribution to the women's widely noted "disposition to keep out of the filds [*sic*] as much as possible." Julie Saville, *The Work of Reconstruction: From Slave to Wage Laborer in South Carolina, 1860–1870* (Cambridge, UK: Cambridge University Press, 1996), 103. Saville cites the following Freedmen's Bureau letters noting this "disposition" in the wake of Emancipation: John A. Smith to L.B. Meunard, Feb. 7, 1866, vol. 128, pp. 217–220, Registers of Letters Received, Columbia, ser. 3155, Subordinate Field Office Records, RG 105; W.T.

Lesesne to Gen. D.E. Sickles, June 28, 1867, M 869, r 14; the quoted phrase appears in A.E. Niles to H.W. Smith, July 13, 1866, Letters Received, Office of the Commissioner, RG 105 [A-7323]. See also Eric Foner, *Reconstruction: America's Unfinished Revolution, 1863–1877* (New York: Harper & Row, 1988), 85.

11. Tera Hunter, *To 'joy My Freedom: Southern Black Women's Lives and Labors after the Civil War* (Cambridge, MA: Harvard University Press, 1997).

12. Jacqueline Jones, *Labor of Love, Labor of Sorrow: Black Women, Work, and the Family from Slavery to the Present* (New York: Basic Books, 1985), 46.

13. Higginbotham, *Righteous Discontent*, 101.

14. Hannah Rosen, *Terror in the Heart of Freedom: Citizenship, Sexual Violence, and the Meaning of Race in the Post-Emancipation South* (Chapel Hill: University of North Carolina Press, 2009), 186.

15. The rules continue:

> 7. All white men found with negroes in secret places shall be dealt with, and those that hire negroes must pay promptly, and act with good faith to the negro. I will make the negro do his part, and the white must, too.
>
> 8. For the first offence is 100 lashes—the second is looking up a sapling.
>
> 9. I do this for the benefit of all, young or old, high and tall, black and white. Any one that may not like these rules may try their luck, and see whether or not I will be found doing my duty.
>
> 10. Negroes found stealing from any one or taking from their employers to other negroes, death is the first penalty.
>
> 11. Running about late of nights shall be strictly dealt with.
>
> 12. White men and negroes, I am everywhere. I have friends in every place. Do your duty, and I will have but little to do. "Outrage in Obion and Logan Counties—Civil Officers Overpowered and the Laws Defied,"*New York Times*, Feb. 5, 1867. (Reprinted from *The Nashville Press & Times*, Jan. 31, 1867.)

16. Rosen, *Terror*, 187.

17. Foner, *Reconstruction*, 200.

18. Francis William Loring and Charles Follen Atkinson, *Cotton Culture and the South Considered with Reference to Emigration* (Boston: A. Williams & Co., 1869); Saville, *The Work of Reconstruction*, 103. See also Foner, *Reconstruction*, 85.

19. Loring and Atkinson, *Cotton Culture*, 15, 4, 14, 20.

20. Hunter, *To 'joy My Freedom*, 27.

21. Hunter, *To 'joy My Freedom*, 27.

22. James, *Shadowboxing*, 58.

23. Jones, *Labor of Love*, 43–44.

24. Jones, *Labor of Love*, 45. Hunter, *To 'joy My Freedom*, 27.
25. The persistence of this ideology throughout the twentieth century is evident in black women's exclusion from public assistance that would allow them to provide caring labor, as black women were considered "employable mothers" and ineligible for assistance. Gwendolyn Mink, *Welfare's End* (Ithaca, NY: Cornell University Press, 1998). Glenn also notes that the WPA functioned to steer black women into domestic labor. Evelyn Nakano Glenn, "From Servitude to Service Work: Historical Continuities in the Racial Division of Paid Reproductive Labor," *Signs: Journal of Women in Culture and Society* 18, no. 1 (1992): 1–43.
26. Teresa Amott and Julie Matthaei, *Race, Gender, and Work: A Multi-Cultural Economic History of Women in the United States* (Boston: South End Press, 1991), 161.
27. "We argue, however, that patriarchy as a system of relations between men and women exists in capitalism, and that in capitalist societies a healthy and strong partnership exists between patriarchy and capital. Yet if one begins with the concept of patriarchy and an understanding of the capitalist mode of production, one recognizes immediately that the partnership of patriarchy and capital was not inevitable; men and capitalists often have conflicting interests, particularly over the use of women's labor power. Here is one way in which this conflict might manifest itself; the vvast majority of men might want their women at homoe to personally service them. A smaller number of men, who are capitalists, might want most women (not their own) to work in the wage labor market. In exampining the tensions of this conflict over women's labor power historically, we will be able to identify the material base of patriarchal relations in capitalist societies, as well as the basis for the partnership between capital and patriarchy." Heidi Hartmann, "The Unhappy Marriage of Marxism and Feminism: Towards a More Progressive Union," in *The Second Wave: A Reader in Feminist Theory*, Linda Nicholson, ed. (New York: Routledge, 1997), 97–123, 104.
28. Rosen, *Terror*, 9.
29. Hannah Rosen, "The Gender of Reconstruction: Rape, Race, and Citizenship in the Postemancipation South" (PhD diss., University of Chicago, 1999), 388–389. Rosen cites *Report on the Outrages Committed by Whites against Blacks From July 1865 to January 1866. Records of the Assistant Commissioner for the State of Tennessee. Records of the Bureau of Refugees, Freedmen and Abandoned Lands*.
30. Rosen, *Terror*, 62.
31. Rosen, *Terror*, 62.
32. Rosen, *Terror*, 62
33. Rosen, *Terror*, 70

34. Rosen, *Terror,* 71.
35. House Reports, "Testimony of Rebecca Ann Bloom," *Memphis Riots and Massacres,* 39th Congress, 1st Session, 1865–1866, Report #101.
36. Danielle L. McGuire, *At the Dark End of the Street: Black Women, Rape, and Resistance – a New History of the Civil Rights Movement from Rosa Parks to the Rise of Black Power,* (New York: Vinage: 2010), xvii.
37. Hunter, *To 'joy My Freedom,* 33.
38. Elsa Barkley Brown, "Negotiating and Transforming the Public Sphere: African American Political Life in the Transition from Slavery to Freedom," *Public Culture* 7, no. 1 (1994): 107–146, 111.
39. Brown, "Negotiating," 112.
40. Brown, "Negotiating," 112.
41. McGuire, *At the Dark End of the Street,* 33.
42. Iris Marion Young, *Justice and the Politics of Difference* (Princeton, NJ: Princeton University Press, 2011).
43. For example, in Tommie Shelby's adaptation of Rawls's theory of justice to dark ghettos he does not fail to note the problem of police brutality.
44. Dominic J. Capeci, "Foreward: American Race Rioting in Historical Perspective," in *Encyclopedia of American Race Riots,* ed. Walter Rucker and James Nathaniel Upton (Westport, CT: Greenwood Press, 2007), xix–xlii.
45. W.E.B. Du Bois, "Marxism and the Negro Problem," *The Crisis,* May 1933, 103–104, 118.
46. "In 1943, 25,000 white workers at Detroit's Packard plant struck in protest of the upgrading of 3 black workers from janitorial service to assembly-line work. One of the worst civil disturbances in history erupted later that year: blacks and whites fought with bricks, bats, knives, and guns, for 40 hours, leaving 34 dead and 100s injured." Nikhil Pal Singh, *Black Is a Country: Race and the Unfinished Struggle for Democracy* (Cambridge, MA: Harvard University Press, 2004), 105, Robin D.G. Kelley, *Hammer and Hoe: Alabama Communists during the Great Depression* (Chapel Hill: University of North Carolina Press, 1990).
47. Hazel V. Carby, *Reconstructing Womanhood: The Emergence of the Afro-American Woman Novelist* (New York: Oxford University Press, 1987), 39. Also see MacGuire, *At the Dark End of the Street.*
48. McGuire, *At the Dark End of the Street,* xx.
49. Cornel West, *Prophesy Deliverance! An Afro-American Revolutionary Christianity* (Louisville: Westminster John Knox Press, 1982), 40.
50. Adolph Reed, *W.E.B. Du Bois and American Political Thought* (New York: Oxford University Press, 1997), 61.

51. Kevin K. Gaines, "Racial Uplift Ideology in the Era of 'the Negro Problem,'" Freedom's Story, TeacherServe©, National Humanities Center, http://nationalhumanitiescenter.org/tserve/freedom/1865-1917/essays/racialuplift.htm

52. "In fact one of the saddest things I saw during the month of travel which I described was a young man, who had attended some high school, sitting down in a one room cabin, with grease on his clothing, filth all around him, and weeds in the yard and garden, engaged in studying a French grammar." W.E.B. Du Bois, Frederick Douglass, Booker T. Washington, *Three African-American Classics: Up From Slavery, The Souls of Black Folk and Narrative of the Life of Frederick Douglass* (Mineola, NY: 2007), 59.

53. Cathy J. Cohen, "Deviance as Resistance: A New Research Agenda for the Study of Black Politics," *Du Bois Review* 1, no. 1 (2004): 27–45, 33.

54. Cohen, *Deviance as Resistance*, 34.

55. Cohen, *Deviance as Resistance*, 35.

56. Susan Moller Okin, *Women in Western Political Thought* (Princeton, NJ: Princeton University Press, 1979).

57. Okin, *Women in Western Political Thought*; Elizabeth V. Spelman, "Woman as Body: Ancient and Contemporary Views," *Feminist Studies* 8, no. 1 (Spring 1982): 109–131; Susan Bordo, *Unbearable Weight: Feminism, Western Culture and the Body* (Berkeley: University of California Press, 1993).

58. Farah Jasmine Griffin, "Black Feminists and Du Bois: Respectability, Protection, and Beyond," *Annals of the American Academy of Political and Social Science*, vol. 568, "The Study of African American Problems: W.E.B. Du Bois's Agenda, Then and Now" (March 2000), 28–40, 29, 31.

59. Griffin, "Black Feminists and Du Bois," 30.

60. Lawrie Balfour, *Democracy's Reconstruction: Thinking Politically with W.E.B. Du Bois* (New York: Oxford University Press, 2011), 100.

61. W.E.B. Du Bois, *Darkwater: Voices from Within the Veil* (Mineola, NY: Dover Thrift Editions), 96.

62. Griffin, "Black Feminists and Du Bois," 34.

63. Griffin, "Black Feminists and Du Bois," 34–35.

64. W.E.B. Du Bois, Darkwater, 96.

65. Griffin, "Black Feminists and Du Bois," 36.

66. Balfour, "Democracy's Reconstruction," 99.

67. Du Bois, "Damnation," 310.

68. Du Bois, "Damnation," 100.

69. Kevin Gaines, "The Historiography of the Struggle for Black Equality since 1945," in *A Companion to Post-1945 America*, ed. Jean-Christophe Agnew and Roy Rosenzweig (Malden, MA: Wiley-Blackwell, 2002), 211–235. Gaines is not alone in reconstructing the racial equality with

reference to "work" and "action" alone. See also Jacquelyn Dowd Hall, "The Long Civil Rights Movement and the Political Uses of the Past," *Journal of American History* 91, no. 4 (2005): 1233–1263.

70. Kevin Gaines, "Racial Uplift Ideology in the Era of 'The Negro Problem,'" Freedom's Story, TeacherServe, National Humanities Center, http//nationalhumanitiescenter.org/tserve/freedom/1865-1917/essays/racialuplift.htm

71. Robert Gooding-Williams, *In the Shadow of Du Bois: Afro-Modern Political Thought in America* (Cambridge, MA: Harvard University Press, 2009), 3–4.

72. Gooding-Williams, *In the Shadow of Du Bois*, 4.

73. Eric Foner, *A Short History of Reconstruction* (New York: Harper & Row, 1988), 124.

74. Foner, *Reconstruction: America's Unfinished Revolution* 283–284. I use the term "formal political participation" consciously, to separate public activities from intimate ones, and to draw attention to the fact that they are both connected to the political order. Therefore, I want to distinguish between activities like voting, or, as Seyla Benhabib has said, "collective deliberation about the good life," and less considered but no less political acts such as "raising one's children well." Seyla Benhabib, *The Reluctant Modernism of Hannah Arendt* (Lanham: Rowman & Littlefield, 2003), 136.

75. Foner, *Reconstruction: America's Unfinished Revolution* 285.

76. James, *Shadowboxing*, 48.

77. Nell Irvin Painter, *Exodusters: Black Migration to Kansas after Reconstruction* (New York: Norton, 1992), 34.

78. Painter, *Exodusters*, 33. Painter states that a single document recorded by Henry Adams and a committee he headed in northern Louisiana most vividly records "the enormity of Black bloodshed between 1866 and 1876:

"The list of beatings and murders enumerates 683 briefly described incidents, and eleven affidavits of about one paragraph each. It includes numerous examples of politically motivated violence in Louisiana parishes:

"164th. Nathan Williams (colored), badly whipped and his cotton taken away without any cause by Bill Mark, a white man, on his place, in 1874, because he voted the Radical ticket.

"228th. Old man Jack Horse and son was badly beat and shot at by white men—they were as bloody as hogs—at or near Jack Horse's place, going to the election November 7, 1870. "333rd. Abe. Young, shot by white men on Angels plantation, spouting about voting Republican ticket, in 1874.

"442nd. Jones (colored), shot about voting a Radical ticket at or near Haynesville, by white men, 1874." Painter, *Exodusters*, 33.

79. Painter, *Exodusters*, 83, quoting Henry Adams in *Senate Report 693*.
80. James, *Shadowboxing*, xx.
81. Kimberlé Crenshaw, "Whose Story Is It, Anyway? Feminist and Antiracist Appropriations of Anita Hill," in *Race-ing Justice, En-gendering Power: Essays on Anita Hill, Clarence Thomas and the Construction of Social Reality*, ed. Toni Morrison (New York: Pantheon Books, 1992), 402–440, 418.
82. Gatens, *Imaginary Bodies*, 71.
83. See Richard Iton's discussion of the racialized "prophylactic/duppy state," Richard Iton, *In Search of the Black Fantastic: Politics and Popular Culture in the Post-Civil Rights Era* (New York: Oxford University Press, 2010), 201.
84. Gatens, *Imaginary Bodies*, 71.
85. Spelman, "Woman as Body."
86. Lisa L. Miller, "Racialized State Failure and the Violent Death of Michael Brown," *Theory & Event* 17, no. 3 (2014): Online
87. Moira Gatens, *Imaginary Bodies: Ethics, Power and Corporeality* (New York: Routledge, 1996), 25.
88. Gates, *Imaginary Bodies*, 71.
89. Thomas Hobbes, *Leviathan* (New York: Oxford University Press, 1998), 7.
90. Gatens, *Imaginary Bodies*, 22.
91. Gatens, *Imaginary Bodies*, 24.
92. Gatens, *Imaginary Bodies*, 71
93. Carole Pateman, *The Sexual Contract* (Stanford, CA: Stanford University Press, 1988).
94. Gatens, *Imaginary Bodies*, 23.
95. Carby, *Reconstructing Womanhood*, 96.
96. Elizabeth Alexander, "We Must Be about Our Father's Business: Anna Julia Cooper and the In-Corporation of the Nineteenth Century African-American Woman Intellectual," *Signs* 20, no. 2 (1995): 336–356, 338.
97. "Each of the essays moves in and out of the first person, fusing a received notion of political theory with the particulars of an African-American and female life. These essays stand in a new space between the first-person confessional of the slave narrative or spiritual autobiography and the third-person imperative of the political essay." Alexander, "We Must Be about Our Father's Business," 338.
98. Anna Julia Cooper, *A Voice from the South* (Oxford: Oxford University Press, 1988), xlii.
99. Cooper, *A Voice from the South*, 60–61.

100. Cooper, *A Voice from the South*, 64.
101. Carby, *Reconstructing Womanhood*, 96.
102. "Angela Y. Davis, *Women, Race, and Class* (New York: Vintage Books, 1983), 128, 133. According to Hazel Carby, "In 1895, the catalyst for the formation of the National Association of Colored Women was a public attack on the immorality of all black women." Carby, *Reconstructing Womanhood*, 39. The Women's Era Club first organized the National Federation of Afro-American Women [NFAAW]. It then took the lead in fusing with the Colored Women's League. In the summer of 1894, the Women's Era Club utilized its journal, appropriately called the Women's Era, to arouse local interest in holding a national convention. The response was positive as many clubs became committed to an 1895 convention.
103. James W. Jack, letter, Mary Church Terrell Papers, Box 102–5, folder 60, Moorland Spingain Collection, Washington, D.C.
104. Josephine St. Pierre Ruffin, "Address to the First National Conference of Colored Women," *Women's Era* 2, no. 5 (1895): 13–15.
105. Ruffin, "Address," 13.
106. Darlene Clark Hine, "Rape and the Inner Lives of Black Women in the Middle West: Preliminary Thoughts on the Culture of Dissemblance," in *Words of Fire: An Anthology of African-American Feminist Thought*, ed. Beverly Guy-Sheftall (New York: The New Press, 1995), 380–388, 381.
107. Hine, "Rape and the Inner Lives of Black Women," 381.
108. Hine, "Rape and the Inner Lives of Black Women," 384.
109. Hine, "Rape and the Inner Lives of Black Women," 379–387.
110. Hine, "Rape and the Inner Lives of Black Women," 380–382.
111. Hine, "Rape and the Inner Lives of Black Women," 384.
112. Cohen, "Deviance as Resistance," 31.
113. Angela Y. Davis, *Blues Legacies and Black Feminism: Gertrude "Ma" Rainey, Bessie Smith and Billie Holiday* (New York: Pantheon Books, 1998), xi.
114. Davis, *Blues Legacies*, 33–34.
115. Davis, *Blues Legacies*, xiv.
116. Davis, *Blues Legacies*, xviii; Daphne Duval Harrison, *Black Pearls: Blues Queens of the 1920s* (New Brunswick, NJ: Rutgers University Press, 1988), 10.
117. Davis, *Blues Legacies*, 5.
118. Harrison, *Black Pearls*, 3.
119. From Ida Cox's "Wild Women Don't Have the Blues," quoted in Davis, *Blues Legacies*, 38.
120. Davis, *Blues Legacies*, 3.

Chapter 4

1. Tommie Shelby, "Justice, Deviance, and the Dark Ghetto," *Philosophy and Public Affairs* 3, no. 2 (2007): 126–161,160. The term "dark ghetto" is taken from Kenneth Clark's 1965 classic work *Dark Ghetto: Dilemmas of Social Power* (New York: Harper & Row, 1965). Shelby is less concerned with how the civic obligations of all blacks are changed by racial bias than with the specific situation of those in areas of spatial poverty. That is my concern as well.
2. Hawley Fogg-Davis, "Theorizing Black Lesbians within Black Feminism: A Critique of Same-Race Street Harassment," *Politics and Gender* 2, no. 1 (2006): 57–76, 64–65.
3. Mick Meenan, "Lesbian Teen Dies in Hate Stabbing: Lesbian Youth, In Droves, Turn Out to Mourn," *Gay City News*, Vol. 2, Issue 20, May 17-23, 2003, http://www.streetharassmentproject.org/news/other/news_gaycitynews.html Street Harassment Project.
4. Charles B. Brack, "Dreams Deferred: The Sakia Gunn Film Project," *The Third World Newsreel: The Queer Essentials Collection*, 58 minutes, 2008.
5. Now Heath Fogg-Davis.
6. Fogg-Davis, "Theorizing Black Lesbians."
7. Joanne Ninive Smith, Mandy Van Deven, and Meghan Huppuch, *Hey Shorty! A Guide to Combating Sexual Harassment and Violence in Public Schools and on the Streets* (New York: Feminist Press, 2011).
8. For informative discussions of these historical and contemporary practices, see Douglas S. Massey and Nancy A. Denton, *American Apartheid: Segregation and the Making of the Underclass* (Cambridge, MA: Harvard University Press, 1993) and Elliot Jaspin, *Buried in the Bitter Waters: The Hidden History of Racial Cleansing in America* (New York: Basic, 2007).
9. Shelby, "Justice, Deviance, and the Dark Ghetto."
10. John Rawls, *A Theory of Justice* (Cambridge, MA: Belknap Press of Harvard University Press, 1971).
11. It should be noted, however, that Shelby believes that if Rawlsian conditions were met, then there would be justice. Specifically, Shelby argues that if Rawls's fair equality-of-opportunity principle were to be realized within the institutions of the wider society's basic structure, this principle "would mitigate, if not correct, race-based disadvantages by ensuring that the life prospects of racial minorities are not negatively affected by the economic legacy of racial oppression." Tommie Shelby, "Race and Social Justice: Rawlsian Considerations," *Fordham Law Review* 72, no. 5 (2004): 1697–1714, 1711. He supports the application of Rawlsian

principles without "radical revisions," as Charles Mills states (Charles
W. Mills, "Retrieving Rawls for Racial Justice? A Critique of Tommie
Shelby," *Critical Philosophy of Race* 1, no. 1 (2013): 1–27.
12. Center for Constitutional Rights, "New NYPD Data for 2009 Shows
Significant Rise in Stop-and-Frisks: More than Half Million New Yorkers
Stopped Last Year," press release, February 17, 2010, New York,
http://ccrjustice.org/home/press-center/press-releases/new-nypd-
data-2009-shows-significant-rise-stop-and-frisks-more-half
13. Center for Constitutional Rights, "New NYPD Data."
14. Elijah Anderson, *Code of the Street: Decency, Violence and the Moral Life of
the Inner City* (New York: Norton, 1999).
15. Shelby, "Justice, Deviance, and the Dark Ghetto," 159.
16. Tommie Shelby, *We Who Are Dark: The Philosophical Foundations of
Black Solidarity* (Cambridge, MA: Belknap Press of Harvard University
Press), 2005.
17. Charles Mills (2007) disagrees about what justice here requires, arguing
that the application of Rawlsian principles alone, without redress, will not
suffice. Although Mills's stance raises important issues, to address them
would go well beyond the scope of this paper. Charles W. Mills, "Contract
of Breach: Repairing the Racial Contract," in *Contract and Domination.*
ed. Carole Pateman and Charles Mills (Boston: Polity, 2007), See also
Charles W. Mills, "Retrieving Rawls for Racial Justice?: A Critique of
Tommie Shelby," *Critical Philosophy of Race*1, no. 1 (2013).
18. I want to note that in an ideal world women and men would share
child-care responsibilities equally, and this would not have to fall under
the domain of women's issues. But we have established that this is a
non-ideal world.
19. Iris Marion Young, *Justice and the Politics of Difference* (Princeton,
NJ: Princeton University Press, 2011), 46.
20. Nikki Jones, *Between Good and Ghetto: African American Girls and Inner-
City Violence* (New Brunswick, NJ: Rutgers University Press, 2010).
21. Jones, *Between Good and Ghetto*, 110.
22. Anderson, *Code of the Street*, 34.
23. Amartya Sen, *The Idea of Justice* (Cambridge, MA: Belknap Press of
Harvard University Press, 2009).
24. Anderson, *Code of the Street*; Jones, *Between Good and Ghetto*.
25. Young, *Justice and the Politics of Difference*. Martha Nussbaum and
Amartya Sen's capabilities approach takes what residents are allowed to
do and to become as its central focus. Beyond their focus on a broad
range of capabilities, with sexual, reproductive, emotional, and affilia-
tive capabilities spelled out in Nussbaum's version, I am also drawn to
their attention to physical disabilities and modifications to primary

goods with respect to such disabilities. I believe this is relevant regarding the issue of violence in dark ghettos, which I address below.

26. Sen states that "primary goods are merely means to other things, in particular freedom" (*The Idea of Justice*, 234. He also states that "the fit between a person's holding of primary goods and the substantive freedoms that the person can in fact enjoy, can be very imperfect, and that this problem can be addressed through focusing instead on the actual capabilities of people," 64.

27. Jael Silliman, Marlene Gerber Fried, Loretta Ross, and Elana R. Gutierrez, *Undivided Rights: Women of Color Organize for Reproductive Justice* (Cambridge, MA: South End Press, 2004).

28. For full elaboration of these injustices, see: Darlene Clark Hine, "Rape and the Inner Lives of Black Women in the Middle West: Preliminary Thoughts on the Culture of Dissemblance," in *Words of Fire: An Anthology of African-American Feminist Thought*, ed. Beverly Guy-Sheftall (New York: New Press, 1995), Dorothy Roberts, *Shattered Bonds: The Color of Child Welfare* (New York: Basic Books, 2003), Jael Miriam Silliman, Anannya Bhattacharjee, and Angela Y. Davis, *Policing the National Body: Sex, Race, and Criminalization* (Cambridge, MA: South End Press, 2002); Anna Marie Smith, *Welfare Reform and Sexual Regulation* (New York: Cambridge University Press, 2007).

29. Dorothy Roberts, "The Racial Geography of Child Welfare: Toward a New Research Paradigm," *Child Welfare* 87, no. 2 (2008): 125–150. Roberts also points out that "researchers have yet to investigate the sociopolitical impact of this spatial concentration of child welfare supervision—the system's 'racial geography.'" (129). Nonetheless, she suggests that one impact is the erosion of trust within the community, a factor relevant for Shelby's solidarity.

30. Deborah S. Harburger with Ruth A. White, "Reunifying Families, Cutting Costs: Housing–Child Welfare Partnerships for Permanent Supportive Housing," *Child Welfare* 83, no. 5 (2004): 493–508.

31. National Coalition for Child Protective Reform, "Child Welfare and Race," issue paper no. 7 (Alexandria, VA: National Coalition for Child Protection Reform, 2011), http://www.nccpr.org/reports/7Race.pdf

32. National Coalition for Child Protection Reform, "Who is in 'The System' and Why?," issue paper no. 5 (Alexandria, VA: National Coalition for Child Protection Reform, 2011), http://www.nccpr.org/reports/05SYSTEM.pdf. See also Ruth Anne White and Debra Rog, "Introduction," *Child Welfare* 83, no. 5 (2004): 389–392.

33. National Coaliti on for Child Protection Reform, "Who is in 'The System?'"

34. Edward W. Soja, *Seeking Spatial Justice* (Minneapolis: University of Minnesota Press, 2010).

35. John F. Kain, "Housing Segregation, Negro Employment and Metropolitan Decentralization," *Quarterly Journal of Economics* 82, no. 2 (1968): 175–197; Sara McLafferty and Valerie Preston, "Spatial Mismatch and Labor Market Segmentation for African-American and Latina Women," *Economic Geography* 68, no. 4 (1992): 406–431; Norman Krumholz, "Urban Planning, Equity Planning, and Racial Justice," in *Urban Planning and the African American Community: In the Shadows*, ed. June Manning Thomas and Marsha Ritzdorf (Thousand Oaks, CA: Sage, 1997), 109–125; Yale Rubin, "The Persistence of Racial Isolation: The Role of Government Action and Inaction," in *Urban Planning and the African American Community: In the Shadows*, ed. June Manning Thomas and Marsha Ritzdorf (Thousand Oaks, CA: Sage, 1997), 93–108.
36. One might note that systems of social reproduction are rarely fair. On the contrary, they impose undue burdens on women. But this is even more so for black women, and state power has been used to skew this system in favor of white women to the disadvantage of black women.
37. There are considerable reciprocity-related issues regarding the gendered division of labor in care provision within black communities. Arguably, due to lack of reciprocity here, black women could refuse to provide care. I think Hirschmann's (1992) gendered theory of obligation, where we recognize that all obligations are not chosen and therefore cannot be regulated by social-contract hypotheticals, is relevant here. Nancy J. Hirschmann, *Rethinking Obligation: A Feminist Method for Political Theory* (Ithaca, NY: Cornell University Press, 1992).
38. Gwendolyn Mink, *Welfare's End* (Ithaca, NY: Cornell University Press, 1998).
39. Roberts, *Shattered Bonds*.
40. They should not, however, join a parallel economy where the gendered division of labor is rearticulated. If Shelby's system is to gain the loyalty of women, it must commit to not recreating the gendered division of labor that obtains in the wider society. I thank Al Tillery for pointing this out.
41. Nancy Hirschmann, *The Subject of Liberty: Toward a Feminist Theory of Freedom* (Princeton, NJ: Princeton University Press, 2003).
42. This is also an issue, though less so, for lesbian and non-gender-conforming women.
43. This issue is addressed within Martha Nussbaum's account of human capabilities and also touched upon in Nikki Jones's discussion of emotional resources surrounding masculine identity for inner-city young men. This issue is difficult to address without strategies to intervene in subject formation, but that does not change the necessity of it from the point of view of justice argued here. I am not sure that Fogg-Davis

adequately accounts for the issue of subject formation in calling for an end to sexist street harassment. Fogg-Davis does make churches and black civil-society institutions the locus of responsibility. I agree that black institutions have a role to play, but they cannot do it alone.

44. Laura Beth Nielsen names street harassment as "a mechanism designed to reinforce [traditional] status hierarchies," and says that many see the issue of sexist street harassment in particular as a response to a world where women enjoy more freedom than before. In this respect it parallels the second phase of sexual harassment outlined by Reva Siegel. This is also important because of Shelby's characterization of the street as legitimate work space. Laura Beth Nielsen, *License to Harass: Law, Hierarchy and Offensive Public Speech* (Princeton, NJ: Princeton University Press, 2004).

Chapter 5

1. Ruth Perry, "Mary Astell and the Feminist Critique of Possessive Individualism," *Eighteenth-Century Studies* 23, no. 4 (1990): 444–457, 454.
2. United Nations Human Rights Committee, "In the Shadows of the War on Terror: Persistent Police Brutality and Abuse in the United States," 31.
3. Beth Richie, *Arrested Justice: Black Women, Violence, and America's Prison Nation* (New York: New York University Press, 2012), 47.
4. Richie, *Arrested Justice*, 97.
5. Edward Soja, *Seeking Spatial Jsutice* (Minneopolis: University of Minnesota Press, 2010), 1.
6. Martha Nussbaum, "Beyond the Social Contract: Toward Global Justice," The Tanner Lectures on Human Values, 2002–2003, 415–507, 503. Martha C. Nussbaum, "The Future of Feminist Liberalism," in *Setting the Moral Compass: Essays by Feminist Philosophers*, ed. Cheshire Calhoun (Oxford: Oxford University Press, 2004), 82.
7. Nussbaum, "Beyond the Social Contract," 448.
8. Nussbaum, "Beyond the Social Contract," 448.
9. Nussbaum, "Beyond the Social Contract," 450.
10. Nussbaum, "Beyond the Social Contract," 451.
11. Martha C. Nussbauam, *Creating Capabilities, Creating Capabilities: The Human Development Appraoch* (Cambridge: Belknap Press of Harvard University Press, 2011), 20.
12. Nussbaum, "Beyond the Social Contract," 448.
13. I have noted above that Afro-Modern thinks have called attention to the threats to black life under racial domination. I want to note here that Shelby is aware of the threats to black life and addresses them specifically

in his article "Justice, Deviance and the Dark Ghetto," Shelby, however, is more attuned to the threats facing black life from state sanctioned violence, including blacks' disproportionate experience of police brutality and murder. He is insufficiently attentive to the threats to life facing the black female subject, where for the last 40 years the black female murder rate has exceeded the white male murder rate. Black women are also twice as likely to be murdered by husbands and four times as likely to be murdered by boyfriends and girlfriends. They are also more likely to be killed in the course of community disputes among other men.

14. Nussbaum *Women and Human Development,* 78.
15. Nussbaum, *Creating Capabilities,* 33.
16. Nussbaum, *Creating Capabilities,* 33-34.
17. Soja, *Seeking Spatial Justice,* 4.
18. Tommie Shelby, "Race and Social Justice: Rawlsian Considerations," *Fordham Law Review* 72, no. 5 (2004): Symposium: Rawls and the Law: 1697–1714.
19. Shelby, "Race and Social Justice," 1711.
20. Shelby, "Race and Social Justice," 1711.
21. Pateman and Mills, *Contract and Domination* (Cambridge: Polity Press, 2007), 131.
22. Pateman and Mills, *Contract and Domination,* 120.
23. Pateman and Mills, *Contract and Domination,* 112.
24. Pateman and Mills, *Contract and Domination,* 108.
25. Pateman and Mills, *Contract and Domination,* 112.
26. Pateman and Mills, *Contract and Domination,* 112.
27. Pateman and Mills, *Contract and Domination,* 131.
28. Pateman and Mills, *Contract and Domination,* 129.
29. Pateman and Mills, *Contract and Domination,* 129.
30. Pateman and Mills, *Contract and Domination,* 129.
31. Pateman and Mills, *Contract and Domination,* 189.
32. Pateman and Mills, *Contract and Domination,* 129.
33. Lisa L. Miller, 2014. "Racialized State Failure and the Violent Death of Michael Brown," *Theory & Event* 17, no. 3.
34. Miller, "Racialized State Failure."
35. Robert D. Bullard, *Dumping in Dixie: Race, Class and Environmental Quality* (Boulder: Westview Press, 2000).
36. D. R. Williams and C. Collins, "Racial Residential Segregation: A Fundamental Cause of Racial Disparities in Health," *Public Health Reports* 116, no. 5 (2001): 404–416.
37. Patrick Sharkey, "The Intergenerational Transmission of Context," *American Journal of Sociology* 113, no. 4 (2008): 931–969, 934.

38. Ruth D. Peterson and Lauren J. Krivo, *Divergent Social Worlds: Neighborhood Crime and the Racial-Spatial Divide* (New York: Russell Sage Foundation, 2010), 50.
39. Sharkey, "Neighborhoods," 6.
40. Sharkey, "The Intergenerational Transmission of Context," 931–969, 934.
41. Patrick Sharkey, "Neighborhoods and the Black–White Mobility Gap," report, Economic Mobility Project, Pew Charitable Trusts, http:www.patricksharkey.net/images/pdf/Sharkey_EMP_2009.pdf, 6, 15.
42. Sharkey "Neighborhoods," 15.
43. Patrick Sharkey, *Stuck in Place: Urban Neighborhoods and the End of Progress toward Racial Equality* (Chicago: The University of Chicago Press, 2013), 45.
44. Richie, *Arrested Justice*, 103.
45. Dominic J. Capeci, "Foreword: American Race Rioting in Historical Perspective," in *Encyclopedia of American Race Riots*, ed. Walter Rucker and James Nathaniel Upton (Westport, CT: Greenwood Press, 2007), xix–xlii.
46. Danielle McGuire writes, "The right of African-American women to defend themselves from white men's sexual advances was tested in the 1975 trial of Joan Little, a twenty-year-old black female inmate from Washington, North Carolina, who killed her white jailer after he allegedly sexually assaulted her. . .The stunning verdict, announced by a jury made up of whites and blacks, signaled the death knell of the rape of black women that had been a feature of Southern racial politics since slavery." Danielle McGuire, *At the Dark End of the Street: Black Women, Rape and Resistance—A New History of the Civil Rights Movement from Rosa Parks to the Rise of Black Power* (New York: Vintage Books, 2010), xxiii.
47. Soja, *Seeking Spatial Justice*.
48. Clare Foran, "How to Design a City for Women: A Fascinating Experiment in Gender Mainstreaming," *The Atlantic: Citylab,* September 16, 2013.
49. Dolores Hayden, "What Would a Non-Sexist City Be Like? Speculations on Housing, Urban Design, and Human Work," *Signs* 5, no. 3 (Spring 1980): S170–S187, S170. (Parenthesis mine).
50. Hayden, "What Would a Non-Sexist City Be Like?," S171
51. Hayden, "What Would a Non-Sexist City Be Like?," S174
52. Hayden, "What Would a Non-Sexist City Be Like?," S176
53. Hayden, "What Would a Non-Sexist City Be Like?," S176.
54. Hayden, "What Would a Non-Sexist City Be Like?," S178–179.
55. Hayden, S175.
56. Hayden, S175.

INDEX

Entries relate to black women unless otherwise noted. Emboldened page ranges refer to chapters.

Printed in Australia
Ingram Content Group Australia Pty Ltd
AUHW010750191023
385138AU00004BA/7